DIG

RONNIE DOSS

ACKNOWLEDGEMENTS

I dedicate this book to the seekers, searchers, and risk-takers. To those that would rather stand alone in truth than conform or compromise. For the overlooked and underestimated that continue to do the work of making our world a better place. To my friends and family that love me unconditionally, I couldn't do what I do without you. Thank you for pushing me to DIG.

PREFACE

"You need an incredible amount of self-confidence to go digging around in someone else's brain." **Dr. Ben Carson**

I can vividly remember the sandbox my Dad built for me out beside our house when I was a kid. My hands and feet would get covered with sand as I pushed little trucks and cars through the yellowish-brown dirt. I would DIG with a small plastic shovel and pour the sand into my bucket. I spent hours and hours by myself, as well as with friends, playing there. Whether it was burying Star Wars figures or making mud pies, there was something about that sandbox that I loved. Digging was one of my favorite things to do. I still believe that digging is an essential part of my life. Of course, I am not talking about digging in a sandbox, I am talking about digging down into my heart and mind to find the things that are most valuable to me now.

Most of us have heard the phrase, *"There is so much more to reality than meets the eye."* Sayings like this help us understand that there is more to life than what appears on the surface. After coaching countless businesses and individuals across eleven different countries, I have learned that there is much more to our lives than we might care to admit. We all have underlying fears, worries, doubts, and concerns that many people will never know about. We must learn to confront them if we intend on building a healthy and productive life.

As I will discuss more in the following chapters, my father

was a brick mason, and I had the great privilege of spending my childhood summers with him on job sites. From watching him work, I quickly began to understand that if you wanted to build something that would stand tall above the ground, you must first be willing to DIG down beneath it. Every home sits upon a foundation of which will determine the long-term stability of the structure. We have almost all seen images of coastal homes on the edge of a cliff crumbling as the foundation beneath them gives way. Beautiful homes costing millions of dollars, and took years to build, can vanish in a relatively short period of time. If we are not careful, all the things we are attempting to construct in our own lives can unfold the same way. We can wind up spending days, weeks, months, and even years trying to correct a faulty foundation that was dug improperly or in the wrong location. Metaphorically speaking, learning to DIG deeper in life can be exactly what we need to become wiser, stronger, and better equipped to leave a legacy to those that will follow us.

Over the years, I've had the great pleasure of visiting some of the world's largest cities and have encountered the skyscrapers that appear to be touching the heavens. The taller the building rises, the stronger the foundation beneath it must be. For us, the foundation is what sustains the weight of life's inevitable, ongoing challenges.

Digging is not only used to create foundations, it is also a process used to create places of protection. Underground facilities like Fort Knox in Kentucky is said to house the world's most valuable collection of gold. This facility is deep below ground and is guarded by military soldiers twenty-four hours a day. The gold that can be found inside was placed there, deep underground, to ensure its safekeeping.

Throughout history, we have chosen to DIG for many other reasons as well. For example, many people DIG to cultivate land. Other individuals DIG to explore. Some DIG tunnels to transport materials from one place to another while others DIG to learn about past civilizations. The planes we fly in and the cars we drive are all fueled by natural gasses that have been pumped out from deep beneath the earth's surface. Those natural resources are available to us only as a result of someone's willingness to DIG. The clothes and jewelry we wear, as well as many of the foods we consume are only available to us for the same reason. Regardless, digging is an essential part of human societies.

As we journey through this book, my hope is that you will be inspired to DIG deep into your own heart and mind to uncover the abundant resources that may have been hidden up until this point. As you discover them, I know you will begin to see your value in much greater measure.

Let's **DIG!**

TABLE OF CONTENTS

CHAPTER ONE
WHO NEEDS TO DIG?

"A champion is not made out of muscle; a champion is made out of heart." **Liang Chow**

I once listened to Arnold Schwarzenegger talking about his early bodybuilding days when he was training to become Mr. Olympia. He shared an instance when someone in the gym lifting weights nearby said to him, *"I never want to be as big as you."* To which Arnold responded, *"Don't worry, you never will."* I find that story amusing because I believe Arnold was clear, even then, that most people are never be willing to do the work necessary to become the biggest and best. He knew that becoming a champion in any endeavor, whether it was bodybuilding, acting, or the political arena would require digging deeper than most people would ever be willing to. He was right!

In this book, as we discuss digging, I will share with you many of the valuable lessons I learned from working with my Dad when I was growing up. My Dad was not an actor or politician like Arnold, he was a brick mason, and to me, he was the best. I can still visit Mt. Airy, North Carolina, where I grew up, and see the homes my father bricked many years ago. I had a terrific childhood where some of my fondest memories are of working with my Dad. I would go with him to work on many weekends and during the summers. I recall those memories quite often. Though it was often sweltering hot during those summer months, it was so much fun just being with him and watching him do what he did so well.

Going to work with my Dad and watching a house being built taught me that, to build anything high, first meant something had to be dug low. I can remember being on a job site waiting for the cement truck to come and pour the foundation for the home my Dad was going to brick. Once the foundation was dug and the cement poured, my Dad could soon after begin laying cement blocks on top of the foundation. Cinderblocks placed on top of the foundation were not as pretty as the fire-red bricks laid on the outside of the home, but necessary to stabilize the structure. Block after block, brick after brick, the house would begin to take shape. My Dad was phenomenal at brick masonry, but what made him great was not merely his skill, but his *passion*. Watching him work was, at times, mesmerizing because he laid down each brick with such care, consideration, and ease. After the completion of each home, anyone who knew to look for excellence in the build, could see that the corners were perfect and the joint lines straight. Observing my Dad laying bricks was much like watching an artist paint a canvas and witnessing a beautiful picture unfold.

I am grateful for all those years of being able to work with my Dad. I gained so much understanding about being a provider for my family, and that down-right hard work is good for the soul.

My Dad said to me when I was a teenager, *"You don't want to do this as your profession. You can be anything you want to be, make sure you choose very wisely."* As a result, I now build people instead of houses.

In the late 1800s, A newspaper interviewed Andrew Carnegie and asked of him, *"Mr. Carnegie, you have over forty men in your employ that are multi-millionaires. How do you find men of that stature to work for you?"*

Mr. Carnegie responded, *"I don't FIND men like that, I BUILD them."* He went on to say that *"Building men is like mining for gold. You have to remove lots and lots of dirt when you are mining for gold; however, you don't go into the mine looking for dirt, you're looking for the gold."*

As we move through this book, I am going to continually reference the idea that we must be willing to DIG deep before we can build anything high. The foundation must be laid, and for that to happen, it must be dug. Digging is a part of growth. Digging is where it all begins, and digging is the key to ensuring what we build will last.

So....

Who needs to DIG?

We all do!

When can we DIG?

Now!

How long do we DIG?

Until!

What will we DIG for?

Better!

DIG!

CHAPTER TWO
DIGGING FOR WHAT?

"The meaning of life is to find your gift. The purpose of life is to give it away." **Pablo Picasso**

If I were to hand you a shovel and ask you to start digging, the first question you would probably ask me is, *"What am I digging for?"*

That question is a vital key to consistently tapping into the energy necessary for any substantial amount of digging. When you have no idea what you are digging for, you will never recognize whether you have found it or not. Or how long you will need to DIG to find it. UNCERTAINTY is a sure path to burnout if it means we have no idea what we are working toward. The reward center of our brain is not engaged when we don't have an end goal in mind. Without that goal, we will never find the fuel needed to endure because we don't have a clear picture of what we are hoping to find.

With that being said, here is a question for you.

Are you clear about what it is you want to discover as you endure each day of this thing you are calling your life?

Let me be crystal clear.

Every day provides an opportunity for us to DIG; with our jobs, our families, our health, and our finances. If you don't know what outcome you are digging toward, eventually the only thing you will have dug is a grave.

I have friends who have dealt with terrible tragedies in life; some have lost spouses because of health issues, others lost children in automobile accidents. If you were to spend time with these individuals, they would remind you through their actions and attitude that the future is never guaranteed.

John F. Kennedy said, *"We must learn to use time as a tool, NOT a couch."*

Most of us have heard the question asked, *"If today were your last day, what would you hope to accomplish?"*

Urgency is **necessary** for any great accomplishment. I have met people from around the world that seem to have waited too long to get clear on what they want to create. It's called regret.

The truth is, it's often not until we lose someone or something we didn't expect to lose, that we develop the urgency to go out and do what we feel must be done. It's a sad truth, but nonetheless, a fact.

In January 2006, I broke both my hands after a hard fall onto a concrete floor. I was in surgery the following day at Northside Hospital where my step-father, Dr. John Hodges, travelled with my mother to accompany me throughout the operation. It was a long day, surgery was complicated, and the recovery process would prove to be even tougher. My mother stayed in Atlanta with my wife Jennifer and myself as my step-father drove four hours back to North Carolina. Upon arriving, he was scheduled to see his podiatry patients the following day. While driving through South Carolina, he began coughing severely and had difficulty breathing normally. A few days later, he was placed on life support and soon thereafter passed away. My step-father spent his 60th birthday in the hospital. While giving a speech at his funeral a few days later, I became aware that it was time to switch career paths and do what I knew I should have been doing all along. Witnessing the hundreds of people my step-father impacted with his kindness, joy, and wisdom, inspired me to work toward reaching the world with a message of hope and transformation. It would be my way of combining what I learned from both my biological father and my step-father.

The loss of my step-father was a catalyst for me getting clear on what I wanted to do with my life. From that time on, I began digging a different path that has led me here, with you reading this book at this moment. This is personal. This is me. A young man from the foothills of North Carolina, urging you to take a good look at your life and start asking yourself some questions that could possibly change everything for you and your future.

So, do you know what you are digging for?

Do you have a clear picture of what you are hoping to find?

Are you truly committed to the thing that you say you are digging for? Or, are you just committed to the *image* of the thing you say you are digging for? There is a HUGE difference. You may need to read the last question again.

Have you considered what your life will look like and feel like once you uncover what you are digging for?

If not, now is the time to take a few minutes and create a schedule that includes "non-negotiable YOU time." This is where you take some time a few days each week, unplugging from all the noise and distractions of life, to clearly visualize your desired future. I am not talking about "daydreaming." I am talking about specific, vivid, imagining. The more specific the picture of what you are digging for, the more clarity and willpower you will have to do the work in finding it. The clearer the image, the stronger the emotion. The stronger the passion, the higher the chance of taking the necessary action of achievement. Digging is about going deeper into your thinking as it pertains to the things you believe you want. Many unfulfilled individuals are ONLY committed to how things appear on the surface. Therefore, they never get to access the wisdom and reward that can only come from the digging deep experience. This is not who you are! You ARE willing to DIG deep and you ARE uncovering more. We can't stop here, there is so much more to be found.

DIG!

CHAPTER THREE
DIGGING PAST MISCONCEPTIONS

"The belief that there is a point when all the material benefits of the world add up to a general state of happiness is the Great Misconception." **Tarek Saab**

MISCONCEPTION: noun: A view or opinion that is incorrect based on faulty thinking or understanding.

Throughout this chapter, I am going to share misconceptions about success that I have learned after working with thousands of people around the world. These misconceptions can keep us from doing the necessary digging to discover more of our highest value.

Jim Rohn once said, *"We are all equal in God's eyes, but we are not equal in the marketplace."* Too often, we don't find success because we have misconceptions about who we are and what we are digging for in the first place.

Here are some MISCONCEPTIONS we must be willing to DIG past:

#1. Success will eventually happen on YOUR timeline.

Wrong! Very wrong.

I once believed that I would be a multi-millionaire by the age of forty, sailing on a yacht in the Caribbean while managing my investments from a laptop computer. My timeline was clearly incorrect! I sometimes laugh at how I once thought I had my life figured out at the ripe age of twenty years old. If I had created all the success I believed I was going to on *my* timeline, I could have retired a long time ago. I was delusional!

The following quote has stuck with me for many years. *"If you think you have already arrived in life, go ahead and unpack all your bags because you are going to be stuck where you are for a very long time."*

Success is a process, not a one-time event. Our timeline is not something that we must adhere to at all costs! Staying open to an everchanging process, and adapting to the never-ending hurdles that **will** appear, is an essential part of attaining our desired destination.

The Universe responds to PURPOSE more than it does PLANS. If we stay on PURPOSE and continue to DIG even when situations and circumstances change, remarkable things eventually happen. Something beyond what we can observe with our natural eyes occurs when we choose to DIG during challenging situations. Even when life doesn't happen how we imagined it would. As the lyrics of the song, "Beautiful Boy," so eloquently states, *"Life is what happens to you while you are busy making other plans."*

#2. Talent is all you need.

Wrong again.

Unrewarded talent is a proverb. Everyone can be great at something, and many people have phenomenal abilities in specific areas; however, this is not enough to ensure success. For example, imagine that you and I were sitting at a coffee shop in Nashville, TN. If we were to look around, I would bet with absolute certainty there would be some incredibly talented artists and musicians close by. Living here for almost five years has confirmed that just because a person has talent, does not mean their success will be guaranteed. Many "starving" musicians are incredibly talented but lack the work ethic necessary to succeed in such a competitive industry. I have heard it said that "natural ability" is often the very thing that keeps a person from doing the "unnatural work" required to achieve greatness.

Tim Notke said, *"Hard work beats talent when talent refuses to work."* You and I could be highly talented. But if we are not willing to DIG past the surface of comfort, convenience, and ease, eventually someone else with fewer capabilities will come along and outperform us.

Legendary NBA basketball Hall of Famer, Magic Johnson said, *"Talent is never enough! With few exceptions, the best players are simply the hardest workers."*

Simply believing that, because you have talent in some area

will ensure you accomplishing great success, is a common mistake. It is time that you recognize just how confused you may be. In a world of competitive business, it is **necessary** to combine talent with a willingness to DIG deep. Even if everyone else is merely leaning on the small, inadequate shovel known as "talent."

#3. Success will always FEEL like success.

Really wrong.

Over past few years, I have done what my friends call, "building an incredibly strong resume." I have been able to work with companies like The Mars Corporation, which happens to be the sixth most valuable private company in the world. The chocolate manufacturing giant produced upwards of thirty-billion dollars in revenue last year. Recently, I was asked to speak to leaders at the headquarters of American Express in New York City and Phoenix. I have trained employees at AT&T, members of the United States Air Force, and have done multiple leadership sessions with teams at NASA. Even though I am now doing exactly what I dreamed of years ago, it doesn't always feel like success. Planning for high profile speaking engagements and training sessions can often be overwhelming. I still get nervous each time I take the platform regardless of who I am speaking to. I was recently conversing with my friend Steve, a successful law attorney of more than 30 years in a suburb of Louisville, Kentucky. He shared with me how, before speaking to a group of people in a boardroom or courtroom, he *still* gets nervous. Even after thirty years of practice. Wow!

Sometimes, when I'm engaged in "robust dialogue" with my clients, family, or friends, it doesn't necessarily *feel* like I am "winning." Having the "heavy" conversations that are required to keep an organization healthy and productive, does not always *feel* like progress. I'm learning to understand that success isn't typically accompanied by feelings of euphoria. Success often presents itself in the form of sweaty palms, a lump in the throat, a nervous stomach and a parched mouth.

My wife Jennifer and I have been together for over 15 years. Our marriage is solid, and we are very much in love. However, having a relationship that works really well does not mean it always feels like it. Many times, we have cried with one another about pains, disappointments, or frustrations we have experienced along the way. We know that *what* gets talked about and the *way* we talk about it determines how our future together unfolds. Everyone desires great relationships, but my experience is that many people won't DIG down past surface-level conversations to address, what could be, underlying issues. Progress is often painful, and success **requires** a willingness to progress, even amid discomfort and adversity. It is not always easy, but when done well, is undeniably worth it.

As you are reading or listening to this, you may be questioning whether or not you have what it takes to be successful. You may be thinking of times when you had a chance to DIG deeper into a conversation or address something difficult for you, but you held back. It is a natural thing to do! On the other hand, we must not allow our misconceptions about success to give us permission to remain "stuck." **Comfort is an addiction**, and digging is not always comfortable. The more we give ourselves permission to pull back when we are uncomfortable, the longer we will remain the same. The longer we stay the same, the more we convince ourselves that the old person we were, is the person we will always be. Digging is our way out of old patterns. Digging is the key to more of what we desire.

Our lives begin to reveal greater rewards at the same pace we are willing to DIG beyond what was once a misconception and embrace new beliefs. Though many people have strong opinions about success, not everyone's opinion has produced the success they pretend to know about. Jesus said it like this, *"You will know them by their fruit."*

#4. The biggest trophies are the ONLY ones that matter.

You guessed it. Wrong!

Imagine you walk into a school where there is a large trophy case standing outside the gymnasium. Would you be more impressed with a trophy case that contained only one tall trophy inside, or one that held many different trophies of all sizes? Chances are, you would appreciate the one that has more. An abundance of trophies, medals, and ribbons would signify many years of participation and achievements in sports and competition. All great coaches and players will tell you that it was the victories as well as the defeats that made them better. Whether it was a "blowout" loss, or loss by a single point, every game played had served a purpose. Just because the trophy earned is not the tallest in the case, does not signify a team's participation was trivial.

When working with clients, whether doctors, scientists, entrepreneurs, or CEOs, I always find out what failures they have experienced in their past and what lessons they've learned as a result. If someone is willing to work with me to aid them in arriving at their next level, then I know they understand how challenging success can be. That's exactly why they are asking for my support.

Legendary basketball coach, John Wooden said, *"Never forget to polish the small trophies because they are the ones that prepare us for the championships."* And just so you clearly understand, Coach Wooden won **ten** NCAA national championships over twelve years as coach of UCLA's Men's basketball team.

Nadia Comaneci, a retired Roman gymnast, is a five-time gold medalist and the first female gymnast to be awarded the perfect score of a 10.0 in an individual routine. She received the perfect score during the 1976 Olympic Games in Montreal, Canada. Considering the countless routines and hours of practice she endured preparing for the perfect 10.0, one could potentially say that she may not have been "that good" of a gymnast. We often don't realize how much effort goes into making a difficult thing look easy. However, she was good, very good! She was called the Queen of the Montreal Olympic games because of her unbelievably sharp routines. Think about it. Ninety-nine percent of her routines were not perfect scores! However, it was the imperfect routines that prepared and developed her into one of the most famous gymnasts in history.

Like Nadia, you and I are being developed each time we choose to get on the mat, the field, or the boardroom. Relocating boxes, sweeping floors, or simply carrying out the trash, all provide opportunities for us to check our perspective, be grateful, and improve. Often, you will DIG deep and still wind up in "second place." Sometimes you will DIG deep and not get the promotion. Sometimes you will DIG deep and again be told "NO." Either way, it's in those times of "not winning the championship" that prepare us for when we will. And if we make it a priority and practice the DIG, we eventually will.

Tim Duncan sums it up with this quote: *"Good, better, best. Never let it rest. Until your good is better and your better is best."*

I want you to recall some of the "small" things you've done along your life's journey and be willing to pat yourself on the back. Be grateful for what you've done, even when things may not have turned out as you had hoped they would. You are learning through all of it, and you **are** getting better.

#5. Success means there will always be applause.

Definitely wrong.

A friend once shared with me an experience he had after working extremely hard to save money to purchase a new Mercedes Benz for himself and his wife.

"I sat at the first stoplight after both pulling out in our new cars, looked up in the rearview mirror, to only see my wife sitting right behind me. I then proceeded to ask myself, "Is this it? Where are the confetti guns and the parade with all the people cheering me on and screaming 'congratulations'!?"

He realized that just because we create a win doesn't mean we will hear the roar of a crowd.

That story has continually reminded me that success doesn't always come with applause. As I have climbed higher and higher on the ladder of success, I have realized, that many times, it seems to get quieter and quieter. It is because of this that many people who become mega superstars often turn to drugs and alcohol to help them cope.

Life is challenging when things aren't going well, but it can also be challenging when things do. A mentor of mine would always say to me, *"You are not blessed by what you get, you are blessed by what you can keep."* If we are working for applause, what happens to us when things get quiet? Praise and criticism are both temporary. But dealing with yourself during the quiet times is a permanent process.

Dad didn't talk much while he was bricking a house. Working alongside him meant sitting in the quiet most of the time. When the greatest painters in the world are doing their job, they aren't talking either. I would bet the same is true for chefs, sculptors, writers, musicians, and surgeons.

I am confident that to remain focused on what we are doing, we need less noise around us as well as within us. Remember, noise destroys! Don't go for applause, go for self-expression. Success is not always loud. We often find the answer to some of life's most difficult challenges when we stop listening to the noise that life is throwing at us and listen closer to the whisper of truth within us. Intentional quiet time is essential to finding the wisdom and truth that may have been within reach all along. We must DIG to find it.

DIG!

CHAPTER FOUR
DIGGING TOO FAST?

"If you want to go fast, go alone. If you want to go far, take some people with you." **African Proverb**

I am an entrepreneur, and as you probably know, I love talking about success in the marketplace AND home. Because of this, the following quote may very well be my favorite quotes of all time, *"Winning in the marketplace but failing at home is failure."*

I am an achiever, and if you are reading this, then I bet you are, too! I wake up in the morning ready to read, write, create, coach, speak, and train. It's who I *am* and who I am *becoming*. I love being a high-output individual. I am passionate about being in the game, and I love achieving my goals. I enjoy checking things off my success list as I go throughout my day. I am actually getting excited just thinking about it. However, and this is a big HOWEVER......

My daughters don't care about payroll as much as I do. They don't care about whether or not I am booked to speak at the next conference or event. They are not concerned with the amount of margin our business creates on a month-to-month basis. They are solely concerned with whether or not I care for them and am willing to spend time with them doing the things they love. Children spell L-O-V-E like this:

T-I-M-E.

Yes, my daughters love that I can buy them nice, fun things, but what I have realized is, those nice things do get old. Toys get put back on the shelf, tossed under the bed, or lost behind the sofa. What **never** gets old is my willingness to pillow fight with them. They love to put on a talent show with my wife Jennifer and myself. We participate as we are instructed, as we are either the audience or the contestants. They never tire of us watching movies together or playing some kind of game. My 10-year-old daughter, Addison, loves for us to watch her do dance moves and gymnastics. Kennedy, our five-year-old, loves for us to watch her play ninja. And just to be clear, I didn't just tell you she was a ninja. Ninjas never really want people to know that they are ninjas. Just saying.

When Jennifer first got pregnant with Addison, and I knew I was going to become a father, I began pondering of all the pressures and responsibilities I would have as the provider and protector of my home. I immediately had greater respect for my parents, as I recalled all the precious times growing up with a roof over my head and food on our table. I remember birthday parties, fishing trips, and my mother buying me a new bedroom suit in high school. So many things I never really appreciated at the time, now looking back, were so terrific. I felt like the expectations were high, and I would have to "keep up."

Over the years, as my company has grown, we have been able to provide well for our girls. Jennifer can stay at home and homeschool our daughters. They have the great privilege of traveling with me to new, exciting places and see so many different things. However, that is not what makes our family work. What makes our family work is the time we invest into our children, face-to-face and side-by-side. We wake up in the morning and kiss on our daughters before they have breakfast. We hug and squeeze on them before they've even had a chance to brush their hair. Jennifer and I will let them sit in our laps and hold them until they get fully woken up. My daughters can walk into my office at any time, even if I am doing a live coaching session with a team. It doesn't happen often, but when it does, I will have them say hello to the group I am speaking with at that time. Family is first, and time is what they truly desire. I have learned that my wife doesn't want bags and bags of cash. She doesn't really care about wearing designer clothes. What she wants is for me to check in with her throughout the day and take a moment to connect.

When a team goes out for an archeological DIG, they often do not use big shovels or backhoes. They use small brushes to excavate the land and make sure they preserve what they uncover. I believe digging at life is much the same. If we get in too much of a hurry, we can DIG right past what the people around us need. Yes, resources like money are important, but money is not the actual requirement for meaningful relationships. Just like the saying goes, *"When you have money, your friends know you, when you don't have money, you will know your friends."*

Growing up, we were not wealthy by any means. I can remember times going to school with only change on the counter to pay for lunch. My parents worked hard on their jobs, but they also worked hard instilling specific values into my sisters and myself. I have never doubted that I was loved or cared for. I have always known, that at any time, I could pick up the phone and call my mom or dad, and they would be there for me. Money can't guarantee that. How often do we see families that pass on considerable resources to a child only for that child to squander the wealth and end up broke, both financially and emotionally?

TIME is the key.

I remember crying so hard on the first day of preschool when my mother dropped me off. I was 4 years old and did not want her to leave me. I cried so hard that she eventually stayed with me for the entire day! She would always make time to go on field trips with my class because I *needed* her to. I know that tough love is important, but gentle love is also. My mom cared for and protected me when I was a young man, and my father showed me how to be strong. The combination of both their love and investment of time helped me to become the person I am today.

Don't DIG so fast that your spouse, children, friends, and family pay for it. Yes, work hard but also work smart. I doubt that on your deathbed you'll wish you had spent more time in the office. As often as possible, DIG down and invest time in your relationships even when you may feel like you don't have the time to spare. You'd be amazed at how life's demands often fall properly into place when we DIG past being rushed and put our focus on what we know is the most valuable thing we have. And just FYI, the most valuable thing is not found on the surface, it's found deep inside the heart.

DIG!

CHAPTER FIVE
TOOLS FOR DIGGING

"Do not wait, the time will never be just right. Start where you stand and work with whatever tools you may have at your command, and better tools will be found as you go along." **George Herbert**

In this chapter, I am going to share with you some of the "tools" that are necessary for us to be willing to DIG more effectively in our lives. Tools are an essential part of any job, and digging is definitely a job. Though it may seem daunting and exhilarating at the same time, digging is part of the job when it comes to the transformation of our lives.

Author Stephen King said, *"It is best to have your tools with you. If you don't, you're apt to find something you didn't expect and get discouraged."*

On that note, do you want to know what I believe is one of the most absent qualities in our society today?

It is the thing that turns average people into extraordinary leaders.

It is what can take a single mother and push her to do what-ever is necessary in making sure her children are taken care of. It's the thing that causes first responders to run *into* a burning building and police officers to kick down the door of a convicted criminal on the run. It's the quality that drives a person to the willingness to confront their deepest, unconscious programming and step forward into a new life of forgiveness and faith.

It's called **COURAGE.**

It takes courage to START A NEW CAREER.

It takes courage to STAND ALONE as you STAND FOR YOUR VALUES.

It takes courage to WRITE A BOOK.

It takes courage to START A FAMILY.

It takes courage to ASK SOMEONE TO MARRY YOU.

It takes courage to RUN FOR PUBLIC OFFICE.

It takes courage to MAKE THE PHONE CALL YOU KNOW YOU MUST MAKE.

It also takes courage to SET BIG GOALS AND DIG FOR THEM.

Ronald Reagan was quoted as he spoke to the United States Marine Corps, saying, *"Many people live their lives wondering if they have made a difference. You courageous men and women will never have that problem."*

In 2009, I was in San Diego, California attending one of my mentor's leadership seminars. During this particular exercise, we were asked to hike upward toward a ledge on the side of a mountain. On the way to the top, we were instructed to pick up a rock that would represent some old "story" about ourselves that we would like to let go of. It was a long hike upward, the path was dusty, and there were plenty of rocks along the way. About a quarter of the way up, I spotted a baseball-sized rock from the middle of the path and chose it to represent my story. Carrying it up was not so difficult at first, but after walking for a while and getting sweaty, the dirt from the rock turned to mud and began to cover my hands and shirt. It was not much, but just enough to annoy me, because I never like to look unkempt.

For years growing up, I suffered from OCD. An obsessive-compulsive disorder that would often cause me high anxiety if things in my life were not where they were "supposed to be" and looked the way I wanted them to look. I always dressed very neatly, kept my room tidy, and even cleaned my family's house many days of the week after I got home from school. I, still to this day, have to be careful of when I get stressed in any way because the old tendency to need everything "straight and in order" can keep me from being present with my family and friends. My mother used to say that my car was always "sterilized enough that you could eat off the floorboards." I believe I used the OCD tendencies well to keep things organized and where I could find what I needed.

The rock I was carrying to the top of the mountain on that warm afternoon represented my old story that, "I had to control everything."

To me, control meant having my clothes lined up perfectly in my closet. My shirts hung in the same direction, pants hung the exact same way, shoes in a perfect line, and ties hung nicely on the tie rack to display an impressive collection. The pictures hung on the wall were always straight, my bed was made, the cushions on my sofa were in the "proper" place, and my office area was arranged perfectly. If not, Ronnie was not "okay." It was exhausting having to wipe up a watermark on the cocktail table or make sure a cabinet was closed in the kitchen for me to be able to relax. The need to control my environment was tiring and frustrating, especially when family or friends would come to visit. Jokingly, my family would call me Schneider. He was the character on the TV show "One Day at a Time" played by Pat Harrington Jr. It was funny, and every now-and-then, my family will remind me of good ol' Schneider as I am wiping down the counter in the kitchen or putting away the dishes.

The need to control my environment by making sure every-thing was in place reflected my need to make everything "look good." I believed if everything "looked good," then I was okay, and if everything was in place, I could enjoy my space. If not, I was not stable.

Carrying this rock was not a big deal until it started causing my hands, shirt, and shorts to get dirty. That was not okay for me. But it was the exact thing I needed to have happen. It reminded me of my **need** to let go of the "looking good" program. I know, it may sound simple to you, but for me, it was not.

After what seemed to be a relatively easy climb, we finally arrived at our location on the side of the mountain, where everyone lined up near the edge of the cliff. There waiting for us was a ropes course instructor wearing a harness around his waist, bolted securely into the side of the mountain. The instructor then asked us one-by-one to step into the harnesses that had been laid out for us next to the path. We were asked to put on the harness, while still holding our rocks, to then checking the person next to us, ensuring their harness was on properly and secure.

This was the beginning of a scary experience for me. First of all, I do not like heights. Not at all! I am not sure why heights bothered me so bad back then, but they did. Putting on a harness so I could hang out over a ledge on the side of a mountain was probably one of the most terrifying situations I could have put myself in. But....I did not have to put myself in that situation, my mentor did it *for* me. This exercise, known as "The Edge," would be a transformational event for me. The simple act of waiting to get to the front of the line, while watching other participants stretch out over the edge of the cliff, to then look down at an almost 300-foot drop, was enough to make me want to vomit. My hands were sweatier than they had been before, and now the mud was getting out of control. I was nervous and dirty. So, I was essentially pissed off and definitely out of control. The exercise was working, and I had not even hung out over the edge yet.

Finally, it was my turn. As the ropes instructor clicked the hook into the loop on the back of my harness, it got VERY

REAL. As I slowly inched my way to the edge of the cliff, I could feel every sign of fear and anxiety show up painfully in every square inch of my body. I was tingling, cold, sweaty, and my stomach was in knots. I began to feel vertigo and could not keep my balance very well. The instructor grabbed me by the arm and continued to walk me out to the ledge. All I kept hearing from everyone around was, *"You can do this, Ronnie. You've got this."*

At this point, everything inside of me was screaming, and tears were beginning to run down my face. I was shaking horribly as the wind came rushing up the side of the cliff and reminded me that I was not in my comfort zone anymore. I felt completely out of control. As I shook, I continued to lean out toward the cliff, feeling the tension from the harness securely latched to the middle of my back. As I leaned out more and more slowly over the edge, I began to literally scream aloud. This was not a scream like at a professional sporting event. This was a scream that was releasing every bit of tension I felt deep down in my soul. And yes, I was still holding onto the rock. I could not let go. I squeezed the rock so hard my fingers turned white. I knew I needed to release it, but it was just not happening. All I could think of was falling hundreds of feet below to my death as I smashed onto the jagged rocks below.

As I was screaming, I felt a bit of euphoria and began recalling the time I had gone skydiving with my friend Brent in North Georgia many years prior. At this point, Brent and I had not spoken in years. But the feeling of the wind blowing against my face reminded me of the sense of falling at 125 miles per hour toward Earth after jumping out of a single-engine Cessna airplane like he and I did that day. I pictured Brent clearly in my mind. And as I recalled the pleasant feeling of landing safely on the ground after the five-thousand-feet parachute ride down, I had enough self-awareness to let go of the rock. I saw it fall until I could not see it anymore.

I did it.

I had let go, even when everything within me was screaming, "hold on!" The ropes instructor, seeing that I had released the rock slowly, pulled me back from out over the edge of the cliff and gave me a hug. He said to me, "You did it!" I cried for the next few minutes as fear and the need to control left my body. It was an experience I will never, ever forget. As we walked back down the mountain to the tour bus we rode in on, I reflected on how, moving forward in my life, **I would not hold onto the things that were trying to control me**. I recognized feelings like jealousy, anger, guilt, and even shame. I thought of times that those feelings had taken over my state of being and how they always left me feeling helpless. If I could let go of that rock as I was hanging over that mountain-side cliff, **then I could let go of the perspective I was having at any moment that provoked me to feel like a victim.**

To this day, when I catch myself starting to feel like a helpless, underqualified victim that is out of control, I think of that rock, and release it. Coming down the mountain later that day was part of the process of reflection that has since helped me to stand firm with COURAGE during stressful and uncertain times.

As we arrived back to our bus, I walked to my seat near the back, reached in my bag to pull out my cell phone, and noticed a missed call from Brent. He left me a message saying, *"Hey bud! Just couldn't stop thinking of you, so I wanted to give you a call. Let's catch up soon."* This was the first time I had heard from Brent in a couple of years. Coincidence? Not a chance.

COURAGE!

When we step out into courage, we send out a signal to the universe that says, **"I am still alive and I will not be stopped!"**

Picking up the phone to call someone that you know you need to call takes COURAGE.

Asking for forgiveness takes COURAGE.

Being vulnerable and sharing with someone how you truly feel takes COURAGE.

Leaving an unhealthy relationship takes COURAGE.

Standing in faith to fix a relationship takes COURAGE as well. Going to the doctor to find out what is wrong takes COURAGE. Just like going to the accountant to finally get your "books" in order takes COURAGE.

We need more COURAGE.

Winston Churchill said, *"Success is not final, and failure is not fatal; it is the courage to continue that counts."*

The next tool that we must carry with us is **CONSISTENCY.**

Hanging over a cliff, letting go of fear, and starting a new journey is terrific, but we must continue to walk along the path every day.

In the early 1500s, the great sculptor and artist Michelangelo carved what is now one of the most famous statues in the world, King David. When asked how he did it, Michelangelo replied, *"I simply removed anything that was not the King."*

In life, we are given one block of marble. What we choose to do with it will determine what we leave behind once we pass on. Before my mentor passed away years ago, he would talk about being a great sculptor with our lives and how it meant we must be cautious with every single cut.

Our words, our deeds, and our thoughts are the cuts that we make into our lives. We must be carefully consistent when we start applying the cuts as we begin working on our personal life's statue. Knowing this, I am aware that I cannot just be kind one time. I must be kind all the time. Knowing this, I am aware that I cannot only exercise once, I must exercise regularly. Knowing this, I am aware that I cannot just show up prepared one time, I must show up prepared all the time. Consistency is the key that unlocks the door to a better life.

Too often, we can fall victim to thinking that everything good can arrive quickly. In the world of Amazon Prime and online shopping, we have become conditioned to believe we live in a microwave society and all you have to do is push a button or two and everything you are hungry for is there for you at a moment's notice, ready to be consumed.

Becoming successful in anything worthwhile is more like cooking a Thanksgiving meal versus throwing something in the microwave. The Thanksgiving meal requires hours and hours of preparation, where the microwavable meal takes only minutes. Nothing of value can be built in only a few minutes. Good, sustainable things take time, and we must put in the time.

We must remember that it is never one cut that makes the statue. It is a continuation of cuts from many different angles, that over time, reveals what was hidden underneath. Chipping away, polishing the marble, and then cutting some more is how the creation beneath emerges. When pressure or stress surface, we have a tendency to take one big swipe at the marble. But this is a sure way to fail.

Saying one thing that you will later regret is like taking a big swipe at the marble.

Quitting a job in a moment of frustration is like taking a big swipe at the marble.

Punishing your child without allowing yourself to calm down first is like taking a big swipe at the marble.

Giving up on your dream just because of a temporary setback is like taking a big swipe at the marble.

Blowing through your savings by making compulsive spending purchases is like taking a big swipe at the marble.

Always remember that the BIG swipes, not the consistent, smaller ones, can cause the most irreparable damage. Measure twice, cut once. Think before you cut and be consistent at it.

When I think of CONSISTENCY, I think of SELF-DISCI-PLINE.

Self-love IS self-discipline. I have a difficult time believing that someone truly loves themselves if they do not have self-discipline. Drinking too much alcohol, abusing drugs, overeating, and speaking negatively about yourself is not self-love. Being around people that do not love themselves is NOT self-love either.

Self-discipline is where you become more committed to developing the better, healthier, happier version of yourself rather than allowing casualness and complacency to run your routine.

Consider this:

If it takes fifteen workout sessions to begin noticing any change in your body, was it the fifteenth session that made all the difference, or was the fourteenth session just as important? Of course, the fourteenth was just as important. And, can you get to number fourteen without thirteen? No. Can you get to thirteen without twelve, eleven, or ten? No. Every single one matters. This is the truth about consistency.

Everyone wants the prize, but only a few are willing to endure the process consistently.

At some point, we must be willing to DIG past the casualness that is driven by our **addiction to comfort** and do the work. Consistency is the tool.

Consistency is the weapon we use to defeat the enemy called MEDIOCRITY.

My mentor used to often remind me that, *"Ronnie, no one benefits when you play small."*

Playing small means allowing immediate gratification to pull me away from what I know discipline should do. Even though instant gratification feels good at the moment, it does not reflect true self-love as consistent self-discipline does.

Pushing away a piece of pizza when you know that eating it will make you feel bad the next day is self-love.

Setting the alarm and getting out of bed early to train your body is self-love.

Reading a book like this one that shares wisdom and insight to help you improve is self-love.

The process of digging is self-love.

Eleven years ago, when I had first been exposed to my mentor's training seminars, I instantly wanted to learn the material. He had flown me to San Francisco, California and hired me while sitting across the conference room table at a resort hotel where one of his seminars was being held. It was the beginning of a complete change of trajectory in my life. I can remember the day like it was yesterday. After arriving back home a couple of days later, I began teaching leadership modules in my living room to stuffed animals that I had bought for my daughter, Addison. I would talk to Winnie the Pooh and the rest of the gang sitting on my sofa about goals, teamwork, and personal development. I spoke to them about commitment, focus, and honesty. I worked with them on their challenges and learned to articulate specific ideas and phrases that I would use in the live seminars I would soon be teaching. It was fun! Different than anything I had ever done before, but fun. I was learning. I would practice, practice, and practice until I could talk for hours without missing a beat on the topics of money, relationships, resentment, and agreements. It took a consistent effort of practice and preparation to be ready.

I have heard it said, *"Practice doesn't make perfect but perfect practice does,"* as well as, *"Practice doesn't make perfect, practice makes better."* Developing a consistent routine may be one of the greatest gifts that you will ever give yourself.

Years ago, when I had a career in the realm of real estate and finance, I would always hear people say, "The devil is in the details." That may be true as it pertains to a real estate contract, but it is also true in how we DO our life. The specific details of how we live our lives day-to-day is where success or failure will become manifest. I always tell people that the devil may be in the details, but so is success.

In Robert Kiyosaki's book, "Rich Dad Poor Dad," he speaks of how the wealthy father-figure in his life became so by being disciplined with his income and not spending impulsively. The father-figure in his life that became poor consistently used money to fuel his need for immediate gratification. Both Dads earned similar incomes, but how they chose to handle their money set them apart in terms of wealth. One became rich, the other became poor.

I recently asked a good friend of mine, who is a financial planner for a large investment bank, what his rules were for his own personal, financial approach to life. I never forgot his response. He stated, *"Before we spend money, we ask ourselves if what we are about to do serves our overall goal. If it does not, then we do not spend."*

It's that type of discipline in the area of finance that has helped him scale his wealth to an impressive level.

If you struggle with consistency in the area of finance, don't think that you have to change it ALL overnight. Simply start by applying a few simple principles around saving and investing. You do not have to save half of what you earn. You don't even have to save twenty percent of what you earn. Start with one percent and then work your way up. The same is true for giving. I believe we should be disciplined with our giving and be generous with our resources. If you have a hard time being generous, start out by giving away one percent of your income to an organization of whose values you align with. Through consistency, you can re-train your brain to not be so controlled by money. Consistency can also help you create more margin in your finances. Having some margin can help you feel less stressed and even more creative with how you use your time and money.

Say this aloud with me: *"Consistency is the key. Consistency is the key. I am daily becoming a better version of me."*

Spending, exercising, reading, and learning all require consistency. We must learn to be consistently consistent, by being consistent.

Here's the third tool we need to have if we are going to DIG deeper into our lives and uncover the hidden riches that lie within us.

This third tool is **CLARITY**.

One of my favorite quotes to share is, *"People don't need certainty, they just need a little clarity."*

As I work with teams around the world, whether in live trainings or live video stream, I hear stories of how many organizations struggle with a lack of clarity and vision. Often, great visionaries struggle with implementing their personal vision, and the team struggles to get clarity on the best way to proceed. Families can experience the same strife. When one person has an idea but is not quite sure how to convey it in an empowering way, a lack of understanding can move in like a fog and block the path of progress. When one spouse thinks one way and the other spouse thinks differently, too often a lack of clarity on how to work together can cause frustration, resentment, and even divorce. Knowing where we want to go is one of the most important things we can figure out as we wake up each day and do life. Progress is the key to happiness and health within an organization, and especially within an individual. **But it's impossible to know if you are making progress without an end goal in mind.**

Lou Tice, founder of The Pacific Institute, used to say that, *"Vividly imagining the end result that we want to produce, along with the emotion that we will experience when it has been achieved, is one of the greatest secrets to success there is."*

I often imagine how it will look and feel when my family and I are traveling the world together producing my company's events, all the while, I am helping millions of people achieve their goals. That clarity is empowering and priceless. Without it, I am not going to move as quickly or efficiently toward my goal.

What do you think could be the benefit of not taking the time to gain clarity? There may be many benefits, but I am certain there is definitely this specific one. **When a person refuses to take the time to get clear on what they want to achieve, they are then giving themselves permission to never fail.** My mentor would say, *"It's the cowards way out."* I am not saying that you must know *exactly* how your life is going to turn out when you are a teenager. I am not saying that you must know your life's purpose in your twenties or even your thirties. However, there must come a time where we unplug from all the noise of life, allowing ourselves to receive the download of ideas readily available pertaining to our purpose on this planet. From there, we must put together a plan.

John F. Kennedy sums this idea up well when he said, *"We must not focus on the past, we must not focus on the present, we must focus on the future, or else we might miss it."*

Unplugging to receive a "download of ideas" may merely be digging deep enough into our being to uncover something we already know and believe, but have somehow forgotten. To *remember* means to RE-member; putting together the members of a puzzle that only we were given the pieces for. If you have ever put together a puzzle, you know the importance of being able to look at the image on the box to assist you in finding and placing the necessary pieces. If you never knew what the end picture was designed to be, you would have a terribly hard time understanding how to arrange the contents.

The beauty of life is being able to be spontaneous. Doing things in the spur of the moment can be exhilarating and exciting. However, if we don't have some sort of clarity on what standards we hold for our behavior, and what the statue we are hoping to create looks like, our spontaneous tendencies can lock us in a prison of regret and disappointment. We all *need* balance in our lives. **But balance is not found, it must be CREATED**. Having clarity gives us a positive mental picture of what we are hoping to create in the first place and the ability to assess what areas we may need to work on.

I recently had the privilege of meeting a gentleman in Seattle, Washington that was attending an event where I was speaking. He was a commercial airline pilot and we had the opportunity to discuss some of the areas in his life where he desired improvement. He said that he sometimes struggles with patience toward himself and is oftentimes hard on himself. I reminded him of his pilot training and how the flight path is, the majority of the time, in a state of adjustment. When the plane gets off course, the pilot or co-pilot makes the proper adjustment and steers the plane to get it back on track. I told him that no one in their "right mind" would crash the plane into the ground, simply because they were frustrated about having to make small adjustments. *Clarity gives us the power to adjust our flight path.*

Clarity is the key.

You might be thinking, "Ronnie, what if I don't have clarity on what I want to do with my life?" Well, I will tell you just like

I have told many people before. Being at a place where you do not have clarity is okay for a while, but **you can't give yourself permission to stay there.** I will tell you this: It's okay to be lost but still moving in the right direction.

Serving is a direction.

Taking a temporary job is a direction.

Moving to a new city to experience some new things is a direction.

Learning a new skill is a direction.

Attending a seminar or workshop is a direction.

If you feel stuck because you don't have clarity, just do something. Even if it's just what you would consider a small thing. As you keep moving, more and more of the path will slowly reveal itself. Don't allow a temporary lack of clarity to keep you from doing whatever you can.

Albert Einstein said, *"Life is like riding a bicycle. To keep your balance, you must keep moving."* Eventually, you will uncover more passion and purpose if you just keep moving. Clarity will come, and clarity is vital.

DIG!

CHAPTER SIX
THE GIFT IN THE DIRT.

"A champion gets up even when he can't." **Unknown**

A seed can have all the potential to produce a healthy tree within it, but not until covered with the dirt, will it grow.

Every great leader I have ever studied or had the privilege of spending time with has had one thing in common. At some point in their journeys, all leaders have dealt with REJECTION.

To arrive at the desired destination in life, we must be willing to make adjustments along the way. We discussed in the previous chapter how pilots are always making adjustments to the flight path. In my life, I can tell you that nothing has caused me to adjust my approach to success quite like rejection.

Years ago, I was invited to speak at a very well-known conference where I was set to share the platform with some very successful leaders and influencers. At the time, I was just getting our company off the ground, and having events scheduled was not overly common. Every invitation meant the world to me, as it still does, but this was an event that I believed would be an accelerator toward our long-term success. This event would mean a greater impact and influence sooner than later. I received an email invite that detailed how much I would be getting paid as well as first-class flight arrangements. This was going to be my "big break." I would be speaking to lots of influencers that would hopefully grab hold of my passion and insight and be able to provide even more opportunities like this one in the future. Even if that didn't happen, I was thrilled about getting to speak to such a broad audience and change some hearts and minds. I began to tell my family and friends about this event and how excited Jennifer and I were that I would be a part of it. We were already imagining what new doors would open and how it could catapult us into our next level.

Have you ever been so excited about something, only for that thing you were hoping for to fall through? If not, let me tell you, it hurts. BAD. About one week after receiving confirmation to speak at the conference, I received a second email stating that I had been removed from the itinerary. There was no real reasoning except that the promotor of the event had decided it was not the right time for me to speak there. Needless to say, I was crushed. At first, I could not believe it. Next, I got sad. Then I got angry. How could this happen? Who has this kind of thing done to them? I had never heard of it, and I did not know how to process it. I spoke to my wife Jennifer about it, and we decided it would be best to respond with a polite email saying that we respected the decision. Reflecting back, I am glad we did.

Not too many days after being released from the itinerary, I received a phone call from my good friend, Marcus. Marcus lives in Houston, Texas and is one of the greatest encouragers I have ever known. On the other end of the line that day, Marcus asked how I was doing. To which I responded, *"FINE."* I did not tell Marcus what had happened as I was honestly still processing my emotions. We chatted for a few minutes longer and then hung up. Just a moment or two later, my phone rang again, and it was Marcus. I answered the phone, and here is what Marcus said to me: *"Ronnie Doss, I just heard a voice telling me to call you back and let you know that you are about to experience something SO OUT OF THIS WORLD that you will know you are on the right track and you must never quit."* Again, my response was *"FINE."* And just in case you aren't aware, when someone tells you they are FINE, it often means that they are **F**reaked out, **I**nsecure, **N**eurotic and **E**motional. Because even with the encouragement that day, I was still feeling "FINE."

I told Marcus *"thanks for the call,"* and again we hung up. It was not even a week later that I received my first email from one of the team members at NASA's Kennedy Space Center. The email was sent to confirm they were going to have me begin training their leaders in a new program called "LION."

I could not believe what I was reading!

What I thought was rejection had simply turned into a bit of redirection. What I once thought was going to be the best thing that could ever happen, paled in comparison to what was about to occur. I was launching (no pun intended) to a whole new level, and NASA was going to help me do it. And, just so you know, the game changes once NASA is on your resumé.

From that point forward, since the rejection occurred and the redirection happened, I always think back to how I had no idea what the future held for me, and I still have no idea what it holds for me now, if I just **refuse to quit.**

As a result of that experience, I feel I have matured past taking things so personal when something doesn't turn out as I'd hoped. Having that "dirt" thrown in my face, so-to-speak, has allowed seeds of faith, commitment, and even forgiveness to grow. I am grateful for the pain I felt back then because it made the experience of succeeding even more beautiful. Since first being invited to Kennedy Space Center, I have been invited back multiple times to work with the teams there, and the support and encouragement of my friends at NASA has been absolutely priceless. I even have a t-shirt with the NASA logo on it that says, "OUT OF THIS WORLD." Crazy how the universe works. UNIVERSE......see what I did there?

I have come to the conclusion that being covered in dirt is often the best way for us to see what we are made of and what we can grow into. In the darkness of being covered up like a seed, we feel secluded, isolated, and alone. Thank goodness that **simply *feeling* an emotion doesn't necessarily make our perspectives into truths.** Being covered in dirt can block us from all the external noise of the world and insulate us from distraction. As we feel the weight of the world on our backs, we realize how much we need other people in our lives to help us lighten some of the burdens. I am grateful for my good friend Marcus that encouraged me during that time, as well as other friends and family who helped me stay positive, in what I felt was such a negative situation. When I was covered up with the disappointment of rejection, my wife never left my side and stayed supportive, just like she has always been. She would remind me that one rejection did not mean the end for me. And this is what I am here to remind you, as well.

Being covered in the dirt of rejection and disappointment helped me to prioritize my life better. Since that time, I have stopped believing that *what* I have scheduled on my appointment calendar represents *who* I am as a person. I have learned to accept who I am whether or not people applaud, approve, or endorse me. The dirt taught me that, and I am forever grateful. Trying to be everything for everyone is exhausting. And if you are exhausted, it is even more challenging to dig out from underneath the dirt that life may throw at you.

Has there been a time when you had dirt thrown at you?

How did you respond?

What did you learn from it?

Has dealing with a rejection ever redirected you into a better situation? If so, that result was because of your willingness to DIG.

I recently watched a YouTube clip of Michael Jordan's Hall of Fame induction ceremony speech. He spoke of how he used disappointments throughout his life and career to be what put the "wood on the fire" of his competitive nature. He talked about his roommate Buzz Peterson being named ACC player of the year when Jordan wanted it to be himself. He said it put Buzz on his radar to outwork and outperform. He also spoke of a time when his coach at the University of North Carolina, Dean Smith, had only 4 of 5 the starting lineup featured on the cover of Sports Illustrated. Michael Jordan was not included. Again, this "put wood on his fire." Even Air Jordan had to learn to use disappointment along the way to become the greatest basketball player of all time.

My final thought for you as we conclude this chapter is the importance of always looking for the positive lesson regardless of the scenario we are facing. Yes, while you are in the middle of a difficult circumstance, it can be challenging to identify; however, is possible. Movies are seen best in the dark. And being covered with dirt may give you just enough darkness to be able to project a clearer picture of a better future. If you are willing to do the work, soon the sun will shine in again, and the seeds within you will begin to grow even stronger than ever before.

Before we move on, I want to share with you anothr quick story that has helped me to stay positive and optimistic, even in the face of adversity.

About a year after I began working for my mentor's training company, I spoke at an event that went really crummy. At the end of the enrollment event, I had come up short. Really short.

Out of close to one hundred participants in the room, I had not gotten very many people to register for our next upcoming event. Enrolling people into our weekend seminars was my job, and on this specific occasion, I had not done my job very well. I emailed my results to the office after the session concluded and went to bed. The next morning, I had to be at the airport really early to fly to another city. While sitting at the gate, my cell phone rang. It was my mentor. He asked me how the event went. Knowing that he already knew the results from the email I had sent in the night before, I responded, *"not very good."* What he said has stuck with me since then. He said in his uniquely squeaky voice, *"Ronnie, you are NOT your results. Refuse to make the people you will see tonight at your next event PAY FOR the result you produced last night. Give them your best!"* He went on to tell me that making a difference in the world was much like being a boxer. He said, *"We must learn to take the hits and keep on fighting."* He was a master at analogies such as these to keep our team motivated. I sure do miss him.

Maya Angelou said, *"You may write me down in history with your bitter twisted lines. You may trod me in the very dirt, but still, like dust, I'll rise."*

Though it hurts, the dirt is a gift. Face it well.

DIG!

CHAPTER SEVEN
WHO ARE YOU DIGGING WITH?

"My idea of good company....is the company of clever, well-informed people, who have a great deal of conversation; that is what I call good company." **Jane Austen**

Previously, we discussed some of the tools needed as we DIG for a more fulfilled life. In this chapter, I want to speak to you about WHO we need to have with us as we DIG. I love this quote I recently heard: *"You can't change the people around you, but you can change the people you choose to be around."*

Community is absolutely necessary if we want to excel. Another mentor of mine said it like this, *"People are like elevators. They will take you up, down, or get you stuck."*

When I first moved to Atlanta, Georgia, I quickly began getting mixed up with the wrong crowd. Even though the people I associated with looked good on the surface, their lack of self-control could have easily gotten me into trouble by merely being around them. Mark, a friend of mine at the time, got busted by an undercover police officer at the training facility where I had been working out. Believe it or not, the undercover officer had worked out with Mark and me on several occasions before he finally arrested Mark for selling him an illegal steroid. It was an insane situation, to say the least! But thankfully, I kept just enough distance from Mark and his other friends that I was never a target. When I arrived at the gym to workout with Mark that day, he never showed up. He had been arrested only an hour or so beforehand. After hearing the news of what happened, I quickly realized that being careless regarding who I spent time with, could cost me BIG TIME. I am confident there were times I rode in Mark's car with him to the gym that he had illegal drugs in his possession. Being new to Atlanta, I was naive. Mark was a nice guy but had gotten mixed up with some of the wrong people. Because I thought Mark was fun to be around and a great personal trainer, I spent more time with him than I should have.

The people we surround ourselves with can drastically impact our thinking. I love being amongst people that inspire me to go higher, and no, I don't mean with drugs. By higher, I mean that being around them helps me stay more motivated, inspired, and focused. I treasure being with people that have great ideas, strategy, and a love for building strong relationships with others. I get the most out of spending time with people that want to make a positive difference in the world.

Booker T. Washington said, *"Associate yourself with people of good quality, for it is better to be alone than in bad company."*

I personally don't like to give my time to individuals that continuously:

A. Stay stuck in the past.

B. Talk negatively about others.

C. Complain about their circumstances.

D. Don't have BIG goals.

E. Avoid learning and growing.

F. Manipulate.

G. Pretend to know everything.

H. Take life too seriously.

It may appear to you that I am too picky in regard to my relationships. But I can assure you that knowing the type of person I want to spend my time with has helped me avoid wasting it. Spending too much time with people that don't help me accomplish the "bigger picture" can rob me of the opportunity to serve the world better. Yes, everyone deserves to be loved, but that does not mean I have to spend my time with everyone either. Though it may sound selfish, I decided long ago that I wanted to make a difference in the lives of as many people as I could. And that would not happen if I wasted my time with people that had already decided to go nowhere further than they already were. Many people *want* to stay stuck. People may not directly shove you off course, but they will slowly nudge you off course over time if you are not careful. I refuse to allow a casual approach to my relationships to impact my future negatively.

You may have heard the quote, *"Show me your friends, and I will show you your future."* It has been shared so many times that it would be difficult to know exactly where the quote origi-nated. In the Old Testament of the Bible, the writer said it like this, *"Evil company corrupts good morals."* Being human, we are all impressionable. Our brains are ever-changing and adapting to what we perceive. The mirror mechanism in our brain that causes us to yawn when we see someone else yawning can also cause us to behave like others are behaving.

Psychologists often debate, which is more important, "Nature or Nurture." Nature being our genetics, nurture being our environment. Both are essential contributors to our development, but as we get older, what we are continually exposed to deter-mines what we think and feel about our world. Neuroscientists are now revealing research done over the past few years in the study of epigenetics. Epigenetics pertains to gene behavior based on things that we expose ourselves to. What we eat, where we live, how we exercise, and even who we interact with can pro-duce chemicals that turn specific genes "on" or "off." The genes then tell cells how to behave. If something we are exposed to in our environment turns off genes that attack cancer, then our in-ternal health could be being determined by what we are facing externally. The same is true for our mental and emotional health. If you allow yourself to be around people that rub you the wrong way with their negativity, judgment, or criticism, over time, you may become cynical, judgmental, and critical as well. And if you are a nice person that does not want to hurt anyone's feelings by saying "no," you will easily get caught up in a group of well-intentioned people that may not have your best interests at heart.

Choose your friends wisely.

Association is perception, and perception is a reality. Throughout our lives, we will be judged by our behavior, but we will also be judged by the people we spend time with. My friend Kevin always says, *"Be careful of who you walk in the door with."*

A casual approach to life can result in us having to place our hopes and dreams on hold while we sort out the DRAMA that was created during times of poor judgment. Remember, failure often happens gradually, gradually, gradually, then suddenly. Never wait until your boat has sailed too far down a lousy river for you to decide it is time to get out and make some course correction. Choosing to cut ties with someone that is going nowhere is not rude, it is **wise.** As author Henry Cloud says, *"Boundaries are blessings."*

BOUNDARIES *often produce more results than effort.*

If you avoid establishing clear boundaries in your life, you will spend so much of your energy making very little progress. The drama that we allow into our lives because of a lack of boundaries can become a distraction that hinders us from striking strong and true with our daily goals.

We can love people from a distance, and there is absolutely nothing wrong with distancing ourselves from people that are toxic or dysfunctional, even if those people are family or past friends. Jennifer and I are grateful for our families. We are fortunate to be able to spend time together, laugh together, and encourage one another as we work hard at becoming better in every area. My sisters Crystal and Carolyn are so close that they now work at the same University. I do not think you could separate them if you tried! They are like a tiny gang! They even have their own language. Well, at least it seems like it sometimes. Though everyone in our family is different, we all enjoy spending time together. But that is not always the case when it comes to family. People often share with me how they have had to distance themselves from family members that were simply making poor decisions. It is difficult to do so, but sometimes we must first care for ourselves so we can better care for others. Associating with people that continually refuse to make responsible decisions, even if it is family, can be detrimental.

Some of my fondest memories in life have been of going fishing with Dad and my Uncle, Gary. We would wake up early on a Friday morning, climb in Gary's truck and drive almost four hours north to Charlottesville, VA. The fishing was great, but the laughter and storytelling are what I will never forget. Both Gary and Dad were entrepreneurs and I loved hearing their accounts of interactions with the people they got to work with. Uncle Gary once told me to, "Always take excellent care of my customers and clients." I never forgot that advice. Though I have never been perfect at it, I have always tried to build an active community of clients by doing more than was expected and being available whenever they may need me. Sometimes they reach out to me at inconvenient times, but I know that if I needed them, they would do the same.

Here are a few principles that I always remember when it comes to building community:

1. To have a friend, I must first be a friend.
2. What sound quality I look for in another person, I must be willing to be myself.
3. If I want a seat at the table, I must be willing to bring something valuable to the table.
4. If I want quality people around me, I must be ready to improve my quality by adding value to myself.
5. Birds of a feather flock together, and they also arrive at the same destination.

There will come a time in our days when we absolutely need people. Whether during a career change, a health issue, or loss of a loved one, we will all need people around us at some time or other. I say it like this, *"Be careful who you step on as you climb the ladder of success because one day you might see them again on your way back down."* We may believe that we will never fall down the ladder, but circumstances can occur that we never expect.

Pat Riley, former coach of the New York Knicks, speaks of what he calls "COVENANT." He says covenant is often forged by teams that deal with some sort of crisis together. Losing a valuable team member or dealing with a challenging loss during a critical game can be the crisis a great team uses to forge covenant. He says that the bond can pull individuals together and keep them together as the team moves ahead through victories and defeats.

Families need COVENANT.

Friendships need COVENANT.

Teams need COVENANT.

Spoken or unspoken, we all need to stand for some type of COVENANT. A great question to ask ourselves is this, "What values will I bring to the covenant between myself and others? Also, "How are those values going to be displayed?"

Honesty, honor, non-judgment, and authenticity are just a few that come to mind as I think of the covenants that I have with my family and friends.

Honesty means that I will tell the truth even when it hurts.

Honor means I respect the notion that every person I meet is dealing with struggles and challenges, just from being part of the human condition.

Non-judgment means that even though I may not agree with someone, I do not believe my way is the ONLY way. I can love and care for people that may have different beliefs and lifestyles than I have. Non-judgment does NOT mean I lack opinion. It simply means that I will not allow my opinion to overpower my willingness to be kind and considerate.

Authenticity means that I will be myself and trust that others will accept me or not. Either way, their opinion will not keep me from being true to my values.

Digging deeper into our relationships to build a stronger community is something I believe is right for ALL of us. Human beings are tribal creatures, and we love to be a part of something bigger, whether we admit it or not. I believe one of the biggest threats to our world is when we begin to attack people that may not be in "our community." Attacking a group of people just because they have different values than we do is not a sign of intelligence. No group will ever be perfect at making positive contributions to the world, but I do believe that by identifying what values we want our community to have, we have an anchor to help keep us grounded. When the winds of conflict and confusion begin to blow, we are not scattered. Let's be very clear. Winds of conflict and confusion WILL blow whenever there are massive groups of people together. However, that doesn't mean we should attack and do harm to one another.

To truly develop a stronger, healthier community, **we must stop waiting on the light at the end of the tunnel and simply choose to be the light at the beginning of the tunnel.** We are community and community is US.

Are you a part of a specific community that serves others?

OR

Have you pulled away from others because of hurt or disappointment?

Our first response to pain is often to pull back and isolate ourselves. Many times, we can isolate ourselves from family, friends, and community because someone in that particular group did something that we perceived as wrong. Isolation can be deceptive and dangerous! Having a community around you means there are people you can talk to when you experience difficult times. I often say it like this, *"What doesn't get expressed becomes suppressed, what is suppressed becomes depressed, and what is depressed eventually becomes toxic."*

Toxic people hurt people, and we definitely don't want to be that type of person. If you have a large community of people around, or simply a couple of trusted friends, ask them for feedback on how you can be better in that relationship. Ask them how you can serve them better. Feedback is so valuable, and too often we don't ask for it from the people that know us best. The community can offer us valuable feedback and also protect us from other people that may want to do us harm.

It has become clearer and clearer to me that **COMMUNITY CREATES COMMITMENT.** We must be willing to ask ourselves what we are COMMITTED to and then find some people that help us to nurture that COMMITMENT. Often our first knee-jerk response is to pull away from community, but I have discovered that community is essential to healthy growth. We will eventually smooth off some of our rough, immature edges if we DIG past the "isolation impulse" we tend to feel when hurt or disappointed. As a result, we become a more refined, influential leader. If you hang with a weak community, your commitment to a healthier life becomes weak. Community offers us wisdom that we might not have uncovered on our own. It's worth the effort.

Years ago, before my mentor passed away, I remember hearing him say, *"Always protect the herd."* He believed a pack of tigers could defeat a pride of lions in a fight because lions were not used to fighting as a team. Whether or not that perspective is absolutely accurate, I do not know, but the point is a valuable one. We must learn to stand for our community against threats that may appear.

INTERNAL threats to our community could be:

JEALOUSY

UNAPPRECIATION

GOSSIP

UNWORTHINESS

COMPLACENCY

INDIFFERENCE

ENTITLEMENT

LACK OF COMMITMENT

He would often ask, *"Are the decisions you are making in your day to day life adding to the strength of the herd or diminishing it?"* Not taking care of myself mentally, physically, and emotionally was actually taking away from "the herd." Not using company resources well when on a company trip was a form of taking away from the herd. Waiting to book accommodations for travel until the costs became outrageous was a TAKE from the herd. Not listening to a request or feedback from a client or team member was a TAKE from the herd.

He would go on to say, *"It's the small things that we don't do that can mess up the big things that we get to do."* Community is a place where we can not only have support with challenges we may face, but also feel good about ourselves as we support others. Bouncing ideas off of one another and asking for outside perspectives is vital for individuals and communities to grow.

Are you doing the work to bring better resources to your community, or are you waiting for the community to offer you better things? Do you handle things that have been entrusted to you well so that you will always have resources to strengthen your family and community? Or are you operating from an immature, short-sightedness that can put cracks in the armor that you and your family use to fend off enemies? Again, no one is perfect, but I do believe we have a RESPONSIBILITY as members of our community to bring the best version of ourselves to others aid.

I love working with families, corporations, and various types of teams to support them in working together better. I believe it is true; we ARE better together. Ben Franklin said, upon signing the Declaration of Independence, *"We must indeed all hang together, or surely we will all hang separately."*

Now, after a decade of traveling the world and speaking to hundreds of thousands of people, I am clear that the most significant possessions I have are my relationships. The communities I have been asked to be a part of have assisted me in having more creativity, confidence, and clarity. Knowing that I have people I can reach out to if ever needed, and at times I do, gives me the strength to stay in the game.

My challenge as we close this chapter is that you identify and engage in some form of healthy community. Whether that is your TEAM at work, church, small group, book club or recreational sports team, ENGAGE in something that will require you to bring the best part of you. We ALL need it and won't GROW very far without it.

DIG!

CHAPTER EIGHT
PUTTING DOWN THE SHOVEL.

"Life is the continuous adjustment of internal relations to external relations." **Herbert Spencer**

In the last chapter, I discussed how people tend to isolate themselves from a community after they have been hurt or wounded by others. I mentioned that at some point in all of our lives, we would be hurt by others. In this chapter, I want to talk to you about the greatest pain that we can ever feel, and that is the pain we inflict upon ourselves.

Recently while speaking to a group of men in Washington state, a young man stood up in front of the group and shared how cruel he has been to himself. The young man got very emotional as he shared some of the things he often says to himself, even as early in the day as when he first wakes up. He said he "severely judges himself" and tells himself that he is unattractive, unhealthy, and basically undeserving of a good life. I could see the pain on his face as he chose to be so vulnerable.

To begin, we got familiar with the dialogue he was having with himself. I said to him, *"You must be willing to shift from the critical character you have created, to a more affirming character that will serve you."* I then challenged him to look in the mirror and say to the negative character, *"Enough is enough! No one is listening to your opinion anymore!"* I then reminded him that he was powerful, deserving, and worthy. I also reassured him that he was loved beyond what he could even comprehend. This may sound a bit cliché, but being willing to speak to yourself positively is a key to having a quality life. As I have said many times, *"The quality of our life is simply the quality of our internal dialogue."* If we do not get control of how we speak to ourselves, we will never have power of our emotional state. It's not **what** we see. It's what we **say** about what we see that counts.

I am not saying we should allow ourselves to become delusional or blind to the corrections we can make with ourselves, our routines, and our lifestyles. However, when we allow our initial perspective to determine our internal dialogue, it can cost us our joy and peace of mind.

You may be wondering why we are so hard on ourselves in the first place. I believe it is because we perceive the world around us as a scary, confusing place. As a result, our brains work hard to find anything it can find to focus on. Because what we see on the outside is scary, there is a high tendency to make up something similar on the inside. One way we gain some control is to make up a story about how we don't "measure up," and then place our focus and energy on that. Focusing on what we think we cannot do and how we may not be equipped to perform, provides a form of subtle permission to stay where we are. When things around us appear scary, the natural response is to "freeze" and do nothing.

Over the years, I have learned to focus on the solutions I can create instead of the inadequacies I believe I have. In some ways, it's the focal point that we put our creative energy into that fuels our behavior. So, if I deplete my energy by yelling at or talking down to myself, I keep myself "safe" from encountering the uncertain, outside world.

This form of misery becomes a safety mechanism in two ways. First, it gives me permission to not have to achieve great results. Second, it allows me to beat myself to the punch before other people can hurt or disappoint me. For the sake of safety, I can tell myself that I am not a great leader and then cower back into invisibility. That way, I don't have to deal with the pains that could come by opening myself up to others. This is why people who tend to complain a lot use their negative emotions to try and get attention, sympathy, and acceptance from others that are also dealing with a harsh world. Adopting a negative view of ourselves can give us permission to act as if we are disempowered, when we are not.

I titled this chapter, "Putting Down the Shovel" because that is precisely what I believe you and I must do to stop digging at ourselves. I know of countless stories where someone has allowed a past event to cause them to develop a negative story about themselves. As a result, when things got tough, or pressure came as they tried climbing to the next level in a relationship or career, they would self-sabotage and fall back into old behaviors and routines. Doing so would reaffirm the old belief and give them the much needed "certainty" and feeling of control. I call it the "ninety-nine-yard dash." This dash is where we run really hard to prove something to others, only to get right to the end of the race and do something that keeps us from proving ourselves wrong about our negative beliefs. You may need to read over that one again.

We can screw up our relationships, health, or careers in a matter of minutes by allowing ourselves to make choices that do not serve our better selves. Therefore, we reestablish mistaken identities we have chosen to adopt. If this is you, it's time to put down the shovel. Throughout this book, we have discussed the many positive sides of digging. But with this type of digging, there is truly no benefit, other than telling yourself you are **right** about your old BS story.

Telling yourself that no one loves you is a BS story.

Telling yourself that you are not valuable is a BS story.

Telling yourself that there is no way you can create excellent results is a BS story.

Telling yourself that you are unattractive or undesirable is a BS story.

Telling yourself that the universe and the rest of the world are against you is a BS story.

Telling yourself that because you grew up poor, you will never have wealth is a BS story.

Telling yourself that it's your parent's fault is a BS story.

And again, the only benefit we get from telling ourselves a BS story is the feeling of being "right" about it. Even if the thing we are "right" about makes us miserable. **Either you can be right, or you can be happy.** It is time for you to put down the shovel.

I've heard it said, *"If you find yourself in a hole, the first thing you need to do is stop digging."* Many of us have dug holes in our lives because we failed, were rejected, hurt, or disappointed. For the sake of safety, our brain has assessed those events and tried to develop ways of never having to experience them again. We speak to ourselves in unhealthy ways, hoping it will help us avoid the past experience again. Allowing ourselves to eat too much "comfort" food or spend money irrationally in efforts to mask negative feelings is another way of being unhealthy. We lash out at loved ones when they have done nothing wrong, and as a result, WE DIG A HOLE. All of these things are unhealthy.

Graves are holes, and if we are not careful in the pursuit of being right, we DIG graves that we eventually live our lives in. The mess we end up in is often a result of many small digs that we have taken at ourselves and others as we navigate the trials of life. We become our own worst enemy when we take small digs at ourselves, using the verbal daggers of negativity, stabbing them into our own hearts. Will the negative voice go away? No, but we can dilute it with the sound of self-love and compassion.

We must realize that we, just as all other creations on this planet, are deserving of love." When we DIG at ourselves, we are not operating with self-love. In fact, we are almost trying to punish ourselves for not being, having, or doing something we think we should have done. It's a vicious cycle.

When we DIG at ourselves, we begin to feel exhausted. When we take "digs" at ourselves, we are essentially "shaming" ourselves for not being at a level of success we decided in our past that we should be. When we use words like "should," we are not focused on creating what we desire, we are merely reacting to what is already present. The word REACTIVE and the word CREATIVE are the exact same words except the letters are just rearranged. Instead of resisting what you see and saying, "It should not be the way it is," why not ask yourself, *"What have I already created?"* as the positive platform to build from? Where you are currently is not WRONG, it just may not be RIGHT where you had hoped you would be. That is OKAY! Focus on creating new, versus reacting to the old. Below are some signs we are digging at ourselves:

1. When we DIG at ourselves, we become exhausted.

I meet people all the time that are exhausted from their silent battles. When a person resists where they grew up, how their parents raised them, how much money they had, the resistance consumes them. Resistance leads to bitterness, and bitterness can wreck our peace of mind. Maybe our parents didn't raise us per- fectly. Or maybe there wasn't a surplus of money lying around the house, but that does not mean our parents were not doing the best they knew how to do. I tell people all the time, ***"If you are going to blame someone, blame them well."*** When you blame well, you say, *"Because of them, I chose to be courageous, kind or ambitious."*

For example: *Because* of the abuse or neglect you felt grow- ing up, you choose to be loving and attentive to your spouse and kids.

We can always turn the negative into a positive, but when we resist it, we spend our time wrestling what was, versus construct- ing as the architect of what could be. **What you resist, persists.**

2. When we DIG at ourselves, we lose motivation.

When I first began traveling with my mentor, I remember him saying to me, *"Ronnie, if you ever wake up and can't find any motivation, it's because you're being selfish."* What he meant by this was, if I am not looking at the world and recognizing all the opportunities for me to develop solutions, it's because all I am thinking about is my own comfort. I am likely only focused on my house, my cars, and my bank account versus creating so- lutions for others. If we are really committed to **being** a solution to the world's challenges, we will always find motivation, simply because there are so many problems. Remember, challenges are actually opportunities in disguise. Commit to becoming a problem solver, and you will find motivation, even in the most obscure places. Zig Ziglar said, *"Many people say that motivation doesn't last. To which I respond, neither does bathing, that's why we recommend doing it every single day."* When you find an issue and decide to solve it, you will remain motivated.

3. When we DIG at ourselves, our self-confidence diminishes.

It's hard to remain confident if you are always criticizing yourself. Especially for your past mistakes, or what you are doing right now.

Here's a News Flash: **YOU DO NOT ALWAYS HAVE TO BE CONFIDENT TO BE SUCCESSFUL.**

You can work hard, be bold, and stretch for your dreams even while you are scared to death. John Wayne said, *"Courage is when you are scared to death but willing to saddle up anyway."*

I love being around people that are confident in themselves. However, I know that all of us struggle in some areas. For example, a person may be super confident with their management skills but lacking when it comes to interpersonal relationships with family and loved ones. Some people are confident with their time management skills but lacking in their public speaking skills. You can have confidence in your physical appearance but not in your intellectual capacity. As we discussed earlier in this book, confidence is not a born attribute, it must be developed with consistency. It must be worked at. Theodore Roosevelt said, *"Each time we face our fear, we gain strength, courage, and confidence in the doing."*

The first public speaking talk I ever gave was in a small conference room in Atlanta, GA. There were about ten people in the room, and I did a forty-five-minute presentation on a direct sales opportunity. I remember three things about the event. First, I was *really* nervous. Second, I had a parched mouth and a hard time keeping my tongue from sticking to the top of it. Third, I talked really, really, really fast. I did not enjoy the presentation, but the people in attendance did. Some people said, *"Wow, you talk fast, but I can tell you are excited about what you are sharing."* If I had decided never to speak again, simply because I didn't have a lot confidence, I would never be where I am today. CONFIDENCE will come! **FEAR fades when we are willing to do what it takes regardless of the emotion.**

I would admit that I am a much better speaker than I was twenty years ago in Atlanta, but it definitely did not happen overnight. I have hammered away at my craft thousands and thousands of times, and as a result, I have more confidence than ever before. You must refuse to allow yourself to be overly critical of what you are observing. Always be gentle with yourself, monitoring and making adjustments to your internal dialogue. Remember, none of us were born experts in any area. That includes you! Don't allow a previous lack of confidence to keep you from future possibilities. **Every expert was once an amateur.**

4. When we DIG at ourselves, our routine begins to reflect a lack of courage.

A person that is continually digging at themselves will eventually begin to lose courage. Courage leads to boldness, and boldness leads to action. If we are going to speak to ourselves negatively if we "fail," we will always look for ways to minimize risk and avoid ANY potential failure. We then start trying to convince ourselves the best way to ensure decreased risk is to stop taking action all together. By not taking any action, we end up wrapping ourselves in what I call the "immediate gratification blanket." The blanket gives us short term comfort but eventually leads to long term regrets.

It takes courage to stand up to your enemies, but I believe it takes even more courage to stand up to yourself. If you confront the negative self-talk and cut it off as soon as it begins, you will be much more prone to courageousness. Ben Franklin once said, *"Many men die at twenty-five but are not buried until they are seventy-five."* When our courage dies for any reason, mainly because we speak negatively to ourselves, our hopes and dreams begin to die as well. The good news is, if we start to speak life into ourselves with compassion and kindness, our courage begins to live again as well.

Would you speak to a friend or family member the way you speak to yourself? If not, it is time to put down the old, familiar shovel of self-abuse and pick up the new one of self-love, self-respect, and honor. It's a better shovel, and the foundation you DIG with it will support a much stronger, healthier life for you and the people you love.

DIG!

CHAPTER NINE
DIGGING OUT

"If you are digging a hole in the wrong place, making it deeper will not help." **Seymour Chwast**

In the last chapter, we concluded with the idea of picking up a different shovel. I said that the shovel of self-love, self-respect, and honor could help you to live a healthier, happier life. I believe we all want a better quality of life, but what we are currently experiencing may not be that. In this chapter, I am going to discuss how we will all find ourselves in situations where we must DIG out. Some of the conditions we encounter are of our own doing, others not so much. But either way, we must deal with them.

Albert Camus said, *"In the depth of winter, I finally learned that within me there was an invincible summer."*

Wow. What a powerful quote to grasp.

I was attending college at NC State University when I first felt the wrath of a kidney stone. I will never forget lying in the emergency room of a Raleigh hospital after hitting the floor in pain only an hour or so earlier. I was sick, scared, and in a lot of pain. I had no idea what the problem could be, but one thing was for sure, this was going to suck. A few hours into the ordeal, my mother showed up in the ER to check on me. She immediately knew what the problem was. My mother had personally fought the same battle many times before when she was younger. She could feel my pain. Kidney issues caused me to take a medical withdrawal from college that year and kept me from re-enrolling later. During the time I was off school, I decided to move to Atlanta, Georgia, where I would begin my entrepreneurial career. It was a decision that changed my life forever. Though I have dealt with kidney issues for the majority of my life, I promised myself that I would never allow the frustration or discomfort to stop me from pursuing my goals. There have been many nights of emergency room visits and hospital stays as a result of my kidney issues.

In no way do I feel that I deserve an achievement badge for overcoming some of those issues because I know I have a responsibility to provide for my family. And let's face it, kidney issues are definitely not the worst health issue I could have to deal with. Every day individuals are diagnosed with different forms of cancer and various other diseases that may or may not be curable.

For example, a year and a half ago, friends of ours took their young four-year-old daughter, Caroline, to the ER after complaining of stomach pain. What they found out would be life-altering for the entire family. After some scans and blood work, it was discovered that Caroline had stage 4 neuroblastoma. A tumor had wrapped around her spine and was causing horrible pain. It was the beginning of a long, challenging year-and-a-half of

80

chemotherapy and radiation. There were times that we feared the worst. The persistence and resilience of Caroline and her family inspired all of us to keep our lives in check and keep the right perspective on our own life's issues. I am thankful to say that after all of the hospital stays and treatments that Caroline is now officially cancer-free! Incredible!! I have two young daughters not much different in age than Caroline, which caused the situation to hit even more close to home. It is terrific seeing Caroline with her beautiful family getting back to more normal life and begin doing the things that other families may so easily take for granted. They were willing to keep digging, even when adversity pushed hard to stop them.

I could share many stories of persistence and determination that have impacted and inspired me over recent years. For example, my niece Ashlynn, along with her parents Zach and Tarah, have overcome extremely challenging circumstances with Ashlynn's health. Five years ago, Ashlynn was born with a condition called "Turners Syndrome." There are fewer than 200,000 US cases per year. One of the symptoms of Turners Syndrome is heart defects. After having heart surgery in a Texas hospital at only three weeks old, Ashlynn's lungs collapsed, resulting in brain damage. Many complications have occurred since then; and still to this day, the whole family continues to press forward. Zach, Tarah, and Ashlynn are incredible examples of strength and perseverance.

My friends Kevin and M'Lisa in Phoenix, Arizona continue to dig even after being dealt a tragic blow many years ago. One night, the family was involved in an automobile accident, resulting in the death of their nine-year-old son, Brandon. Kevin and M'Lisa, along with their two other sons, Austin and Bryant, have continued to push forward even after such a difficult situation and continue to make a positive difference in the lives of others. They have used their heartache and pain to help others find faith amid tragedy and loss. It is hard to explain the contribution they have made in my life and the life of my family.

Any time I begin to complain or have a negative attitude, I can think of how my friends have overcome much more challenging circumstances than I have had to face and use the example of their perseverance to shift my perspective. All of us can tend to have a negative attitude at times, but we also have something called **CHOICE** to help us find the proper attitude. Finding the right attitude helps us to keep digging forward and deeper. There are other stories of perseverance like these I have just mentioned that have helped me keep my perspective in check and press on. You may know some also. Digging out of tragedy, difficulty, and setback is what truly makes people stronger.

Albert Einstein said, *"Adversity introduces a man to himself,"* and Benjamin Franklin said, *"If it hurts, it instructs."* To grow, we must deal with pain. In all of the training I have done around the world, I have never heard anyone say, "I loved the pain." However, I have heard many people say, "It was during the pain that I grew the most." To grow, we must be willing to DIG.

Hardships are often the starting point for change. Many people never change until they have to deal with stresses that expose some disfunction or underlying issues. My mentor used to say, *"Every choice we make has costs as well as benefits; and most of us will not change until we see that our behavior is going to cost us something that we are not willing to pay."*

For example, avoiding financial matters can eventually throw us into a situation of which can be difficult to DIG out. In a recent podcast interview, the host asked what I believed was a key element to success. My immediate answer was PERSISTENCE. I shared how, when I first started my company, there were absolutely no guarantees. I said with confidence how "I did not give myself a plan B." As I began to get my company off the ground, there were times when we were not sure how we were going to make it. As I have shared many times, we lost a lot of possessions along the way, but we refused to quit.

We dug in when other people might have retreated. And it has taken us many years to DIG out of the hole that was formed. Financially, we went through it! We had cars repossessed, almost evicted, and I totally screwed up my credit and got behind on my taxes. It is overwhelming to think about and can laugh about some of it now, but it was surely not so funny back then. I know what it feels like to speak at an event, sharing positive, leadership, and mindset principles while feeling so anxious about some area of my own personal life. We would pay hundreds of dollars to the bank in NSF fees each month because our outflow was higher than our income, so our upkeep almost became our downfall. **But still, we kept digging.**

I vividly remember returning from the first training I ever did with American Express to get home and find an American Express credit card I had applied for sitting on the counter. It was a significant accomplishment for us because we had known what it felt like to struggle with our credit. High-interest rates and expensive penalties had wreaked havoc on us during previous years when there was not much cash flow. Being able to say that I have spoken for American Express, and to see an American Express in my wallet, is something of which I am very proud. It surely has not always been that way though! Digging out of financial hardship is one of the many challenges that we can ALL face. Using the difficulties to learn how to manage our resources well is one of life's most valuable lessons. Remember, it is the pressure on a piece of coal that eventually produces a diamond. We must DIG even when we are feeling the pressure.

I remember when I was younger hearing someone say that if you DIG far down enough, you will eventually come out on the other side of the Earth. Even though that would be a lot of digging, the principle has always stuck with me. When you face obstacles, keep digging.

Years ago, my mentor was asked by a mortgage brokerage to come and work with their team. The owner of the company said, *"If you don't help us get this turned around, then I'm bailing out."* I will never forget my mentor's response as he said, *"Then I am not willing to help you."* Perplexed, the owner replied, *"What do you mean?"* My mentor went on to explain, *"If bailing out is an option, then I don't think you have what it takes to lead your team."*

It reminds me of the NASA missions where they say, *"Failure is NOT an option."*

I have grown enough personally and professionally to know that **failure IS, in fact, an option** in relation to our growth as human beings.

We must not spend our lives running from things just because of the chance we could fail. However, we WILL fail. As we have discussed earlier in the book, we all fall short, but there is always light at the end of the tunnel if we will just keep digging for it. As with the mortgage broker, would my mentor be willing to work with you if he were still alive? Would he ask you enough questions only to uncover that you have given yourself the option of quitting? Remember, I said the reason I succeeded is that I did not give myself a plan B. Maybe some people try multiple things before they become successful, and I actually think that is a beneficial idea. What I do not think is a good idea is giving ourselves an "out" once we have found what we know is our purpose in life. We must identify our purpose and DIG forward, allowing our gifts and talents to be developed and expressed.

In the animated Pixar classic, "Finding Nemo," Ellen De-generes plays Dory, a fish that is helping another fish find his son, Nemo. The story is entertaining and heart-warming. During one of the scenes, Dory tells the dad, *"When you are having a hard time and feel lost, just keep swimming."* It becomes a catch-phrase that the movie is known for and has stuck with myself and countless others, reminding us not to give up. In this book, we say, *"Just keep digging."*

When the road is hard, and the future is uncertain,

just keep digging.

When they walk out of your life or do things to hurt you,

just keep digging.

When you want to quit and take the easy way out,

just keep digging.

When you wonder why you started digging in the first place,

just keep digging.

When the money is tight, and the stresses are high,

just keep digging.

When "they" say bad things and assign false motives to you,

just keep digging.

When your fingers are dirty, and your back is tired,

just keep digging.

When no one is watching, and you feel alone,

just keep digging.

You are coming out on the other side, and you are making way for others to do the same.

In your own life, who are some people that have just kept digging even amid difficult circumstances?

What qualities did they exhibit during those times? How and when have you done the same?

Watching other people's examples of persistence and determination can give us the inspiration and motivation to keep digging when we want to quit. Observing other people can push us to DIG deep within ourselves and obtain the strength to keep digging out. Even when everything within us is yelling, "STOP!" Digging past this threshold, that is at first causing us to panic, is a necessary part of any great achievement.

Before we move on to the next chapter of this book, I want to share with you a module that I often teach in our one-day EMERGE seminar called, "The Threshold." In the module, I explain that there are typically four responses to the threshold that we will all eventually encounter if we dig toward a big goal.

The first response is to STOP.

What many people do not realize a form of stopping is, is to appear "busy." I learned years ago from one of my first mentors that "busy" and "productive" are two very different things. One way we stop pushing through the threshold is to "be busy" doing things that do not move us closer to the goal, but actually, become a diversion attempting to alleviate the discomfort we feel when on purpose and pushing forward.

BUSY is a fast track to MEDIOCRITY.

Another way to "stop" when we experience the threshold is to play "confused." When we are confused, we tend to use that as an excuse to stop doing anything other than nothing. Many people say, "When you don't know, do nothing." However, I think that is a copout. If you are reaching for the stars, there will be times when you are not clear on exactly what to do, but you MUST not allow that to cause you to quit. Ask some questions, research the topic, find the answers, but do not get off track just because you don't have all the answers yet. None of us do. As I said earlier in the book, EVERY expert was once an amateur.

Are you playing confused or making yourself busy doing menial tasks to keep you from doing what you KNOW you need to do to press through the threshold? "Busy" and "confused" are diversions from the task at hand. So is pretending to be "sick" or "too overwhelmed." Both can be diversions as a response to the threshold. I always say as I am teaching this module that, "We must be honest enough to call ourselves on these BS responses if and when they occur." STOPPING doesn't always mean literally STOPPING. Sometimes it just means we have STARTED engaging in a different behavior that temporarily numbs our discomfort with distraction.

Read that line again.

The tendency to numb the pain we begin to experience as we approach the threshold becomes an "easy way out."

The second response to the threshold of hard is to RETREAT.

Retreating is where we default back to a time in our lives when we had some measure of success or acceptance. For some people, it may be middle school, high school, or even college, and what they were doing back then becomes a safe haven for delusions of grandeur. The "GLORY DAYS" mentality offers a temporary rush of excitement as they think about how "back in the day" they were "winning at life." Many people get out into the real world for the first time after leaving the safety of home, only to get kicked in the teeth by a (sometimes) cruel world. As a response, the individual will retreat into the cocoon of the past and begin exaggerating the details of who they were back then, and how, *"If coach had put me in, we would have taken state."*

(Paraphrasing Uncle Ricco from the movie, "Napoleon Dynamite"). The same guy who said he could, *"throw a football over them mountains,"* and spent his days videotaping himself pretending to be a quarterback and throwing passes to no one.

Our fashion choices, our car choices, our love interests, and even our hair style can reflect this unconscious RETREAT mentality. Unlike the first response I described, RETREATING often takes us back even further into the past and can deceive us into believing that we are winning, when in reality, we may not even be in the game anymore. The good news is, **there is still time left on the clock if we are breathing.** Don't be Uncle Ricco. Push past the threshold called RETREAT.

The third and seemingly most enticing response to the threshold is, JUMPING TO THE SIDE and STARTING SOMETHING NEW.

Jumping to the side means we simply move away from the threshold of the previous goal and put ourselves into a completely different situation. One where we won't immediately experience any pressure, discomfort or adversity. When we jump into a new relationship, everything is amazing. It is fun, exciting, and passionate. Starting a new job can be the same way! Running after a new goal is the same way in the beginning. This response is what I call it becoming a "goal hopper." You've met this type of person before. A goal hopper wants to be a hairstylist in January, an engineer In February, and by the end of the summer has tried a couple of other careers, including videographer and truck driver. Who knows, by the end of the year they will have decided to become an astronaut or tattoo artist as well. Either way, the goal hopper never has to deal with the pressure of the threshold for very long because they won't stick with anything long enough to *feel* it. Yes, on the surface these people may be fun to talk to for a few minutes, but if you DIG beneath the surface, you will typically find an empty, shallow vessel, filled only with excuses and justifications as to why nothing else ever worked.

The outcome of the "hopping" behavior doesn't seem to faze the career hopper, though. He or she will continue to jump around when things get difficult, keeping the unproductive pattern alive. People do it with relationships, careers, diets, and health routines. They can do it with jobs and spiritual pursuits as well. The song and dance of avoiding the threshold becomes exhausting for **everyone** involved. So, it may be time to stop hopping around and start DIGGING **in**. I could go on, but I won't. Not with the "jumping off to the side" at least. I am going to push through to the next response, as this is the **ONLY ONE THAT WORKS** when it comes to creating growth and personal success.

The fourth and final response to the threshold is: DIGGING IN and PUSHING THROUGH.

Not stopping, retreating, or jumping off to the side, but PUSHING THROUGH. This is the one that decides it all! PUSHING THROUGH separates "the men from the boys", "the women from the girls," and the "leaders from the followers." It is the vetting process of the Universe. The threshold is the filter, and the only thing that can get to the other side is a person willing to DIG in and endure the process.

The threshold is the breaking point where most decide to pack their bags and go home. It's the point in the trail where most hikers will choose to turn back from the climb and seek lower ground. Like Navy Seal training, the threshold is where people throw up their hands and quit by ringing the bell. Pushing through the threshold reveals the best-of-the-best and typically compensates individuals both mentally and monetarily. The threshold is where champions are formed!

The threshold comes in many forms at many times, but we *know* when we are experiencing it. It hurts! It whispers in our ear that we "don't have what it takes," and it pushes against our very being to see if we truly are committed to getting through to the other side. **The threshold feels like our enemy, but on the other side we realize that it was our friend.** As one of my friends who served in the military once told me, *"You hate your drill sergeant when you're training for battle, but you love them when you're taking off your gear after returning home from the war."* The threshold is that drill sergeant. The threshold is that thing that makes you better.

It might scream at you, push against you, or call you ugly names, but it CAN and WILL make you better if you don't stop digging. The threshold will help us understand what we can become if we will choose to lower our heads, tighten our bootstraps, saddle up, DIG down, and push through. Any person calling themselves a leader must learn to move TOWARD the threshold during uncertain times, instead of running FROM it.

Every great geographical discovery in history has come as a result of pioneers and explorers pushing beyond the temptation to quit, even when there was uncertainty. Bad weather, low rations, sickness and disease, as well as potential attack from an enemy, could have easily caused those individuals to abort their expeditions. Fortunately for all of us, they pressed on into uncharted territory. Christopher Columbus, Jacque Cousteau, Vasco Di Gama, Lewis and Clark, and many other great explorers staked their claim-to-fame in the history books by never allowing the threshold to STOP them. Instead, they allowed it to DEFINE them.

Other individuals like Martin Luther King, Gandhi, Abraham Lincoln, and Winston Churchill did the same. If we want to arrive at our next level, NOT continuing to DIG is no longer an option. STOPPING, RETREATING, JUMPING TO THE SIDE or any response other than DIGGING IN and PUSHING THROUGH, must not be considered. Our growth into the next level demands it!

Today is the start of a NEW season that will become what we make it. Let's keep moving.

DIG!

CHAPTER TEN
GROUNDBREAKING CEREMONY

"It was character that got us out of bed, commitment that moved us into action, and discipline that enabled us to follow through." **Zig Ziglar**

In many cultures and traditions, a GROUNDBREAKING CEREMONY is an event that signifies the beginning of a building project. The ceremony often creates a buzz around the community, letting everyone know that a project of construction has officially begun. In attendance at these ceremonies may be community leaders, politicians, or dignitaries. Persons in the community affiliated with the project are often invited to participate, as a shovel or shovels are placed just above the ground at the building project site. It can be an exciting day for a community, in hopes the new structure will provide professional services or conveniences to the area. These new projects may represent an abundance of jobs and opportunities for people living close by. Many times, the structure being built represents a new season of growth and change for this particular region or country. Groundbreaking ceremonies are simply meant to signify A NEW BEGINNING.

Companies will often go to great lengths planning for a Groundbreaking Ceremony, as it can be used as a personal touchpoint with clients and customers to say, "You are a part of this effort." Marketing for the event can be used to cast vision and build anticipation for the coming days ahead. Vision and anticipation are what gives the individual holding the shovel incentive to DIG down. As with any person hoping to build something new, there must be a vision for the end result and the excitement to do the work.

What is vision?

Vision, as it pertains to goals and productivity, is the thing that we use as the picture of what can lie ahead. Vision is our imagination at work, compiling images of positive feelings and outcomes that will manifest when we are willing to DIG in step-by-step to complete the job. The more specific the vision, the more powerful the pull toward the end result.

Steve Jobs said, *"When you are working toward your purpose, you don't have to be pushed, the dream pulls you."* And, it was Albert Einstein that said, *"Imagination is simply the preview of coming attractions."* He also said that, *"Imagination is more important than knowledge because knowledge is limited; imagination is not."*

Vision is about what you see before anyone else sees it. It is the ability to see into the realm of the unseen and unknown. It is the ability to forecast potential results long before the work to produce those results has begun. Groundbreaking Ceremonies are the expression of vision and the first step in the actual building process. Without vision, it is difficult to start anything great.

VISION gives us perspective, and perspective gives us POWER.

I often tell the story of a man that walked onto a job site where a brick mason was laying bricks. He asked the man what he was doing, to which the mason responded, *"I am just laying bricks."* The man then walked down to the other end of the job site where another man was laying bricks. The man asked the other mason what he was doing, and he had a very different response. The second brick mason responded with a look of excitement in his eyes and said proudly, *"I am building a palace!"*

Both men doing the same job. One had a vision, one did not.

Vision is what compels us to DIG when others are only satisfied with what they already see on the surface. In a world full of surface-level players and shortcut finders, the willingness to consistently DIG into vision is a quality not often seen.

DIG day is the NEW "D" day. It is the day we become so Disgusted with what we already have that we Decide to Dig Down and Develop the Disciplines necessary to arrive at a better Destination. This "D" day represents the Groundbreaking Ceremony for the future you are going to build.

A BETTER business.

A BETTER career.

A BETTER relationship.

A BETTER health routine.

A BETTER spiritual walk.

Anything you have decided to embark upon, today can be the day.

Why not allow today be the groundbreaking ceremony for Y-O-U incorporated?

I can vividly recall a few moments of time sitting in a hotel room in Tacoma, Washington, almost seven years ago. I knew it was time to hit the "send email" button on my computer that would notify my mentor's company of my resignation. I sat staring at the computer screen, knowing that when I hit "send," it would be the beginning of a new season. One filled with much uncertainty and hardship. It was clear that things were not going to improve if I neglected to do what I knew I had to. My stomach was turning, my hands were shaking, and my heart was racing as I hesitantly hit send. Just like that, it was on its way. I know you can't un-pop popcorn, and just like that, the popping had begun. It was a bittersweet moment that I will never forget. From that moment, my wife and I began to DIG in a brand-new way. By hitting that send button, I immediately moved from being employed to now a solo entrepreneur. If I would have known how challenging it would be, I maybe wouldn't have sent that message; however, I knew I had to. Visionaries often do not understand all the complexities involved with their vision coming to fruition; they only have a picture of the outcome etched in their heart and mind. You and I do not need to know all the ways that this new building called "ourselves" will take shape; we simply must be willing to break the ground and begin a brand-new work.

Walking away from an abusive relationship may be necessary for you to build a stronger, healthier self. If this pertains to you as you're reading or listening to this, stop what you're doing, pack your bags and walk out the door. Once you do, NEVER look back! Crossing the threshold of the doorway you exit through can be the Groundbreaking Ceremony of your NEW life. Leaving the old life behind may seem scary for you at first, but it will provide a better, safer, healthier place for you to live and grow. You deserve that! No one should ever remain in an abusive relationship.

Actor Terry Crews speaks of times as a child where his mother packed their clothes into trash bags in preparation for leaving Terry's abusive father. Terry wet the bed until he was a teenager, out of fear that his father was going to come home and beat him and his mother. His story is powerful and portrays a horrifying situation where a young family was traumatized by ongoing abuse. Terry said that his mother would get to the door, even walking outside a few times, only to turn around and go back inside because she didn't know where else to go. Too often, people that don't know what to do, stay paralyzed by fear, and cause others to pay the price. I have never been in a situation like Terry's, but I have heard from enough individuals who were willing to DIG down and push beyond uncertainty in order to create a better future for themselves and their family. It is what must be done!

Farmers must DIG the soil in order to plant new seed, all the while understanding that good seed won't grow in the wrong soil. It may be time for some new soil in your life.

Having a tough conversation with a member of your family or team can be a Groundbreaking Ceremony.

Signing adoption papers or your wedding license can be a Groundbreaking Ceremony.

Writing the first word of a new book can be a Groundbreaking Ceremony.

Doing the first pushup in a new workout routine can be a Groundbreaking Ceremony.

The key is, don't wait for life to plan your ceremony for you. YOU create it!

You may not have anything specific in mind right now that can signify a Groundbreaking Ceremony for you. And that is entirely okay. I am aware that some of the scenarios I mentioned before regarding abuse at home or in the workplace are extreme. However, they are meant to remind you that no matter how difficult a situation may be, we can always begin to DIG out.

Your situation is probably completely different, and I am sure it is. And maybe you are on top of the world right now crushing your goals. Awesome!! But you cannot stop digging. **Winning is no excuse to stop digging.** Even if you are ahead in the race to success, you will eventually get run over if you just sit still. As I have studied success, personal development, and teamwork over the past decade, I have heard countless stories of companies that were once on top in their respective industries, later finding themselves struggling to stay afloat. These giants of industry begin laying off employees and closing down locations to stop the bleeding. Many times, it was too late. Circuit City, Toys R Us, K Mart, Brookstone and many others that once reigned supreme, are now almost extinct.

Athletes and A-list actors that were once winning prestigious awards can, like those mega-corporations, begin a downward spiral from the mountaintop. Without the courage to take risks, make adjustments, and keep digging, these individuals can soon be placed on the infamous "Where Are They Now?" list. It is unfortunate to see a person that was once dominating in some area of life hit rock bottom. How do we avoid this? The only way I know of is to keep digging when things may be going great AND when things are not. Digging at all times keeps us moving forward.

Just because someone has hit bottom does not mean they can't DIG their way out and end up even higher than they were before.

Henry Ford said, *"Failure is simply the opportunity to begin again more intelligently."* And to me, beginning again more intelligently signifies we have dug beyond what was once a place of failure and mined out valuable insight along the way.

I have said it before, and I think it is worth repeating here. *"Wisdom doesn't just come from experience; wisdom comes from reflected experience."* Looking back at the down times and asking ourselves the right questions can assist us in designing a plan for our future, and for that, have a Groundbreaking Ceremony.

So here is my question for you as we DIG ahead:

Are you willing to pick up a few different shovels, so that you can not only continue digging, but also dig better than you ever have before?

At almost all Groundbreaking Ceremonies, the shovels are already provided. All the participants need to do is show up and reach for the one designated for them. When it comes to our personal Groundbreaking Ceremony, we will have to bring our *own* shovel along with us. In the next chapter, I will discuss different types of shovels. That if you are willing to pick up, carry, and dig with, will not only produce results you desire, but do so more effectively and efficiently. We still have more to go.

DIG!

CHAPTER ELEVEN
THE MOST ESSENTIAL SHOVELS

"Give us the tools, and we will finish the job."
Winston Churchill

Even if we throw a terrific Groundbreaking Ceremony, we still must finish the job. Can you imagine spending time, energy, and resources to throw the most magnificent Groundbreaking Ceremony of all time only to stop there? Can you imagine the disappointment of those in attendance after finding out that the process of the build never progressed any farther than it had on that ceremonial day? What a waste of time and energy! The same applies with life.

What's the point of getting all these terrific insights, if you are only going to remain in the same place of getting yourself ready, only to get ready? Many people spend their lives "getting ready to get ready." They talk about the Groundbreaking Ceremony, mention elaborate plans to build, yet never take it any further. It is great to start a thing, but even greater to finish it. Completion is a quality of the great ones in history. As my mother has said to me many times throughout my life, *"It's not where you start, but where you finish."*

I am pretty sure I am getting a clear picture of who you are, especially if you are reading this far into the book. We are now into the last chapter, and you are still reading, still digging for more. I admire you, and I appreciate you. The words in this book are the vessels that carry my commitment to DIG. Digging for you, digging for me, and digging for others. As you know, this book didn't just appear out of thin air. There were countless hours of preparation and planning for this book to ever take form. You are holding an idea that has taken shape, and hopefully, is spurring ideas in your mind for your future. I would be selling you short if I didn't include within these pages some of the specific shovels that I have personally learned to pick up, carry, and DIG with. These particular shovels often require searching below the surface to find them. In chapter five, we discussed the tools of courage, consistency, and clarity. Here, I will drill down with a few shovels I did not have access to when I first began my personal journey of digging. I learned how necessary these shovels are to be able to DIG personally and professionally in the world of leadership, transformation, and personal development. These are the shovels I carry with me, especially now that I am reaching larger, higher productivity teams and global corporations, as well as building a healthy family dynamic. These are the shovels that DIG out the very best in me as well as the people I work with.

#1. The shovel of **EXCELLENCE.**

#2. The shovel of **HONESTY**.

#3. The shovel of **INTEGRITY.**

#4. The shovel of **INNOVATION.**

#5. The shovel of **INTENTION.**

I waited until the last chapter to share these principles with you because they are honestly the most crucial part of this entire book and I want to finish our time together with you thinking about them. The reason I say that is because it's not just that you are *willing* to DIG; the real question is, *HOW* will you DIG? Will you DIG with the shovels I just mentioned, or will you DIG with shovels that may be easier and more convenient to handle, yet produce a lower quality result? Hopefully, a below-average result is not what you are digging for. As I discuss the different shovels, pay close attention, because I can promise you that using them can be abundantly profitable for you in all areas of your life. And who doesn't want to be more profitable?

So, let's talk about the shovel of **EXCELLENCE.**

General Colin Powell once said, *"Productivity is never an accident. It is always the result of a commitment to excellence, intelligent planning, and focused effort."*

In my wallet right now, tucked away in a compartment behind my driver's license, is the Ritz-Carlton credo card. Some would argue that the Ritz is the finest chain of hotels on the planet. The credo of the Ritz-Carlton is as follows:

"The Ritz-Carlton is a place where the genuine care and

comfort of our guests is our highest mission. We pledge to provide the finest personal service and facilities for our guests who will always enjoy a warm, relaxed, yet refined ambiance. The Ritz-Carlton experience enlivens the senses, instills well-being, and fulfills even the unexpressed wishes and needs of our guests."

The credo card also lists the Ritz-Carlton's Service Values, which at any time, any employee should be able to recite. I haven't been an employee at the hotel for over twenty years, but I still carry the card to remind me of the values that have made this organization successful. Listed below are their service values just as they are listed on the card I carry:

1. *I build strong relationships and create Ritz-Carlton guests for life.*

2. *I am always responsive to the expressed and unexpressed wishes and needs of our guests.*

3. *I am empowered to create unique, memorable, and personal experiences for our guests.*

4. *I understand my role in achieving the Key Success Factors and creating The Ritz-Carlton experience.*

5. *I continuously seek opportunities to innovate and improve the Ritz-Carlton experience.*

6. *I own and immediately resolve guest problems.*

7. *I create a work environment of teamwork and lateral service so that the needs of our guests and each other are met.*

8. *I have the opportunity to continuously learn and grow.*

9. *I am involved in the planning of the work that affects me.*

10. *I am proud of my professional appearance, language, and behavior.*

11. *I protect the privacy and security of our guests, my fellow employees, and the company's confidential information and assets.*

12. *I am responsible for uncompromising levels of cleanliness and creating a safe and accident-free environment.*

I am sure you will agree that these are some solid values. The great thing about these values is that the Ritz-Carlton does not simply have these values hanging on the walls for employees to see. They do the work to make sure the values are written on the hearts and minds of everyone that are part of their teams as well. I know I am continually reminding myself of these values as I grow myself and my company.

And lastly, the Ritz-Carlton motto states, *"We are Ladies and Gentlemen, serving Ladies and Gentlemen."* This simply means that if I am a part of the Ritz-Carlton organization, then I behave as a lady or gentleman would, as I serve both the ladies and gentlemen that are guests, as well as employees. It is a culture that is kept alive and strong with every individual that serves in any capacity there. I can assure you that it is absolutely refreshing to experience this type of service after staying at other properties and frequenting businesses that don't seem to care about whether they serve with EXCELLENCE or not.

If you weren't clear before, you should be now. I am a big fan of The Ritz as well as the values they stand for. So, what does EXCELLENCE look like when it comes to our own personal and professional lives?

Regardless of the company you work for, even if you are self-employed, you CAN and SHOULD do your best to exemplify excellence in every area. Excellence defined is, *"The quality of standing out or being extremely good."*

It doesn't matter if you are a coffee shop barista, server in a restaurant, stay-at-home mom, physician in a hospital, student, or janitor at the courthouse. You, too, can operate with excellence. As a matter of fact, everyone can. Even if you are a long-time employee, or happen to be unemployed currently, you should operate with excellence as you do what you MUST until you can do what you WANT. If you are going to take your resumè to different companies, do it with excellence. Dress up, put on your best, start knocking on doors and making phone calls to the very best of your abilities. If you do, something will quickly shift for you. Operating with excellence in how you speak and dress will set you apart from other applicants. Trust me on this one.

If you are currently working at a company, regardless of your job description, do what you do with excellence. Answer the phone, type out emails, respond to requests, and do it all with excellence. **If you are going to give your time to it, give your very best to the time.**

What do you think sets the best companies apart from the worst, besides the specific product they offer? I will tell you. It is their customer service. How they treat customers and employees is what causes people to want to work for or do business with them. Don't get me wrong, you must be able to deliver a quality product, but you must also learn to offer that product with excellence. Why do I talk about excellence so much? Well, it's because I think EVERYONE enjoys experiencing a product or service that is provided with excellence. Whether that's a tire change, service at a restaurant, or an overnight stay at a hotel. Excellence is a wonderful thing, and it will do wonders for your personal brand if you choose to operate that way. Making an effort to remember someone's name, how you stack merchandise in a store, how you dress, whether or not you show up on time, and whether you choose to put a smile on your face are all signs of excellence. Moving quickly and with urgency is also a sign of excellence. How you keep your office space, your home, and your car are also signs of excellence. Excellence is a standard that raises the experience level of ourselves and those around us.

Excellence is a habit that we develop when we learn to take our life and work very seriously. I could go on, but I think you are getting the picture. Successful organizations, families, and marriages all have the high standards, and so should we. Casualness is a sign that we do not take what we do very seriously. And if we don't take what we do seriously, what does that say about us?

I challenge you to approach your employer or manager and tell them that you are going to work at being more of a person of excellence. Notice I didn't say perfection. Perfection is simply about how something looks on the surface, but excellence is how something looks and how well it works all the way around. If you feel that you are already a person of excellence, ask someone you trust how you may improve. Maybe one small thing can make a massive difference in your career or relationships. I promise you, the higher you go, the more you will need to pay attention to details and operate with excellence. Maybe not in every single area, but as much as you possibly can. As you do better, you will get better.

I recently read a quote that said, *"Excellence is the UNLIMITED ability to improve the quality of what you have to offer."* Think about that. There is an UNLIMITED ability to improve anything that we are doing. That's powerful! That means I can **always** improve at being a husband, father, son, employer, or employee. I can get better at ANYTHING I choose to do. What an opportunity you and I have to be excellent at what we do. Not only in our professional lives, but in every area of our personal lives as well.

DIG!

Next, let's talk about the shovel of **HONESTY.**

Again, on the surface, the subject may seem a bit boring. But living with honesty and learning to speak your truth is anything but that. I've heard it said like this, *"Integrity is telling the truth to myself, honesty is telling the truth to others."*

In life, it's usually pretty easy to find out what is true. However, it isn't typically as easy telling the truth to someone whom you know or care for. Telling the truth when you have messed up is often a difficult thing to do. Not so much because of the words. The words are easy to say. **It is the meaning we place on the response that we believe will happen as a result of sharing them.** Honesty takes courage, and as I mentioned in chapter five, courage is necessary for a successful life.

Learning how to package the truth is a wonderful skill to acquire. Making sure the "plane lands" with someone as it pertains to our words, is an incredibly important consideration. One of the most damaging things someone can do is share what they believe is their truth in an unfiltered way. We have all met someone that was "brutally honest," and no one really likes to work with that type of person for very long. Yes, it is refreshing when someone is truthful. But when a person is not willing to learn HOW to communicate their honesty well with others, it can and often does, become a train wreck.

Consider this. Some things are beneficial for people's minds but not good for their hearts, so always proceed with caution.

Take the time to consider what the truth may do to the person hearing it and share accordingly with their emotions in mind. Learning to use your words wisely when conveying the truth will be an asset to you and your future if you want to be a leader. Leaders need to be respected, and respect will eventually require intentional honesty. It is spoken of great communicators that, *"they could tell you to go to hell, and you would thank them for it."* Both sides will eventually respect an honest person.

In your business dealings, be honest.

With your spouse and children, be honest.

With your customers, clients, and teams, be honest.

With yourself, be honest.

Honesty may require digging beyond what feels comfortable for you, but beneath the surface of comfort is where the most fulfilling rewards are discovered. Dishonesty eventually cracks the foundation of trust upon that of which healthy families and organizations are built. You probably know this to be true in theory, but deciding to live with honesty is an entirely different story. Literally!

We all know someone that exaggerates the truth or avoids it. And many times, that could be you. But honesty will breathe life into your relationships and strengthen the bond between you and the ones to whom you are closest. Even if you don't know someone very well, you owe it to them to be honest. When you are dishonest, you actually steal the other person's right to the truth. When you aren't honest, over time, you will stop respecting yourself because you know the truth. You need to be able to count on yourself just as others should be able to count on you. The truth will set you free, even if it ticks you off at first.

Digging down and being willing to be honest will help you build a life, that in the end, you will be proud of. The truth may hurt, but so do the consequences of lies.

DIG!

Now, that we've beaten the honest truth to death, let's discuss the shovel of **INTEGRITY**.

The integrity of a bridge will determine whether or not the bridge can adequately withstand the weight it was designed to hold. When the integrity is out, things can become very dangerous for those that rely on the bridge. We have all seen or heard stories of bridges collapsing; destroying the bridge, anything beneath it, and hurting or killing those that were on top of it. When we lack integrity in our own lives, we take the risk of damaging our reputation and brand. Our legacy can even be damaged when there is a lack of integrity present.

None of us are perfect. We all have faults and weaknesses, but a lack of integrity shouldn't continually be one of them. I am going to say this next phrase as clearly as any other that I have shared in this book. IF YOU AREN'T GOING TO FOLLOW THROUGH, DON'T SAY THAT YOU WILL.

Trust me when I tell you that your customers and clients will not want to do business with you if you are one of the many people in our society that OVERPROMISE and UNDER DELIVER. You will spend your life trying to recover the clients you lost when you didn't deliver. It's a vicious cycle where everyone loses.

For example, if you can't deliver the goods or services you say you can provide by a specific deadline, then DO NOT say that you will. Nothing will frustrate your client base like broken agreements. My mentor used to say, *"THERE ARE NO SMALL AGREEMENTS."* An agreement is an agreement regardless of how big or small we may think it is. INTEGRITY is what causes us to keep those agreements. If you say you will be there, BE THERE, and if you say you will call someone back, CALL THEM BACK!

Here is a question for you.

What would most people say about you if they were honest?

Would they say you are reliable and operate with integrity, or would they say you don't deliver? Would they say that working with you has genuinely been a pleasant experience, or would they say you have caused them high levels of stress and disappointment? Whatever the answer may be, there is always a good time to start over and build with integrity. I understand that these questions may be uncomfortable for you to answer, but at the end of the day, it is this type of digging that can make us so much better.

I also understand that you cannot make EVERYONE happy. But having a strong track record over time is very attainable and needs to be a high priority for us. Whether we are an accountant, speaker, firefighter, or a pastor, INTEGRITY is IN, and a lack of INTEGRITY is OUT. I personally do not think there is anything more satisfying than creating success and knowing it was done the right way. And to be clear, you know what the right way is. We all do.

DIG!

Now let me share with you what could be the most essential shovel of all.

INTENTION.

For those of you that have never heard me speak on a platform or in front of an audience, allow me to give you a little insight. What I mean by INTENTION, and what other people think INTENTION means, is probably not the same thing. I can almost guarantee it.

To understand why INTENTION is so vitally important, you must first understand how I define the word INTENTION. To me, INTENTION means our **DEEPEST COMMITMENT.**

In other words, you can have multiple commitments, but you can only have one true intention. Intention in its truest form is the thing that produced the RESULT we have right now. It has been my INTENTION to type the exact number of words that are in this book, and we know that because that specific number is what we have. No more, no less. The amount of joy we have produced in our lives so far has absolutely been our INTENTION. Not good, bad, right, or wrong. The result simply is what it is. Are there results that are out of our control? Absolutely! But the results that we ourselves have produced have an absolute specific INTENTION to go along with them. I had an intention to write this book, and the way we know this, is that the words are here on the paper. Without intention, we could not, and would not be able to see anything written. If it were my intention to write only one word, we would only see one word. If it were my intention to be done right now with this book, this would be the last sentence I write. INTENTION is specific, and it expresses itself on a moment-to-moment basis.

INTENTION is observable in the present moment, simply by looking at what has become manifested in its present form. The universe has INTENT, and it is expressing that INTENT every single second. How could it not be? Even if there were nothing, that would be how the universe would be choosing to express itself.

So, let me anchor this down before I take you too far off into the deep end. If you have ever said you were going to do something and didn't, from the perspective I am speaking of, it was

NOT your intention to do it. Your intention was to do or be exactly where you were at that time. If you said you were going to come over to my house and help me move boxes but ended up sitting in traffic trying to get there, your intention was not to help me move boxes. Your intention was to sit in traffic. It is an incredibly simple concept, but at the same time, extremely complex.

CLEAR INTENT, or what I call INTENTION, is the most powerful force in the universe. Clear intent produces exactly what is meant to be expressed at that moment. If the intent is for more, then more must be expressed, or else it would not be what I am talking about. Getting clear on this idea means I am always willing to ask myself what I must have been committed to, based on the results I produced. The intention/deepest commitment is what leaves us with the exact outcome that has materialized in our worlds, before our own eyes. If we have not seen it, then it was not our INTENTION to see it.

When a team says, "It was our intention to achieve a specific goal, but in the end, we did not." I would say it was DEFINITELY NOT their intention. The team's intention was to do whatever they did that produced the result they got. Again, intention matches the exact result. Nothing more, nothing less. When I work with big companies or organizations, this is one of the critical points I drive home. It all starts with intention. Within the context of this book, it is either our intention to DIG, or it is not.

There is absolutely no in-between as far as I am concerned. Understanding what our intention is, and getting that clarity, is the most important step as we start digging for our future.

I had better know what I was committed to before walking into an enrollment event for my mentor's company. In other words, my INTENTION. Did things work out exactly how I had *intended?* Yes! Were the results exactly what I had *hoped for?* ABSOLUTELY not. The difference between what we HOPE FOR and what we are COMMITTED TO, are as far apart as the East is from the West. Beginning to grab hold of this concept shifted how I got clear toward where my intention needed to be focused.

So how does intention apply to each of us, regardless if we are part of a mega-corporation or startup, stay-at-home-mom or working parent, student or unemployed? Whether or not we are achieving what we say we want, how does intention apply, and why will we produce better results once we begin to understand its power?

I will explain.

If clear intent is the seed, our actions are the water that nourishes the seed. On a deeper level, the power that tells the seed what to be, and how it is to express its nature, is clear intent. Clear intent is a force that is expressing itself, at all times, in many different ways. The greatest question is: *will we behave in a manner that allows the result to be expressed through us or someone else?* I believe clear intent is always looking for a willing vessel because each of us has the free will to think, speak, and act any way we choose at any time. Even if the circumstances around you change, you can still choose to stay focused on the things you can control, to allow the end result you want, manifest.

Sandor Marai said it beautifully. *"And yet, sometimes facts are no more than pitiful consequences because guilt does not reside in our acts, but in the intentions that give rise to our act. Everything turns on our intentions."*

Yes, I may say I want happiness, but am I truly committed to it? And if I say I am committed to it, how will I know this is true? The answer....WHEN I AM HAPPY!

Yes, I may say I want to lose weight, but am I truly committed to it? And if I say I am committed to it, how will I know that is true? The answer.... WHEN I LOSE THE WEIGHT! Not when I *begin* exercising or change my diet. ONLY when I have lost the weight will I know it was my INTENTION.

Yes, I may say I want more intimacy in my marriage, but am I truly committed to it? And if I say I am committed to it, how will I know that is true? The answer.... WHEN I HAVE MORE INTIMACY IN MY MARRIAGE!

A person might say their INTENTION is better physical health. But what their intention really may be is to waste their time, not meal prep at home, and end up eating fast food instead. The RESULT they produce will have a matching INTENTION connected to it somewhere.

The person that says they want more intimacy in their marriage may wish to have it, but they may be more committed to working all the time, being stressed out, or never investing into their marriage emotionally and psychologically. The RESULT they produce will have a matching INTENTION connected to it somewhere.

So, what is your INTENTION as it pertains to:

YOUR FINANCES?

YOUR HEALTH?

YOUR MARRIAGE?

YOUR RELATIONSHIP WITH EACH OF YOUR CHILDREN?

YOUR CAREER?

YOUR DAILY ROUTINE?

If you refuse to get clear on your INTENTION, then everything becomes permissible for you. When I learned to get clear on my intention and dial it down to as many specific areas as possible, the quality of my relationships, work, and my life as a whole got better. Why? Because that was my INTENTION.

Talk to your teams at work about intention. Talk to your

spouse and children about intention and then take some time being as specific as you possibly can about what RESULTS you are
committed to creating. It will give you a more precise picture on
what matters to you as an organization, family, and individual.
Getting clear on our intention is like being given a specific road
map that can lead us to a beautiful destination.

And lastly, remember that if you do not set the intention for
your life, the intention will be set by default through situations
and circumstances that occur.

**Do not be frustrated with the results you did not produce
with an INTENTION you did not set.**

NOT setting an intention is an INTENTION in-and-of-itself.
Read this over and over again until you gain full understanding.
You will find that the universe punishes the vague but rewards
the specific. Make your request known and do the digging to allow it to manifest.

DIG!

And finally, let's talk about the shovel of **INNOVATION.**

When I think of INNOVATION, I am talking about the process of altering, reorganizing, and revolutionizing the way things
are done. It can be a new method, product, or idea. Innovation is
allowing what could be next to take shape in our lives. What is
next can only develop after we become open to newer, better

ideas. There are different types of innovation. There is both incremental and disruptive innovation. Regardless of type, all involve allowing NEW to spring forth. It is never enough to have a new, innovative idea if there is no follow-through to see it take shape.

I have heard it said, *"There are two guarantees in life. Number one, change is happening all the time. Number two, almost everyone resists it."* Why are people so prone to resisting change and avoiding innovation? Is it a lack of resources, a lack of knowledge, or just plain old complacency? Maybe it's all of the above.

Or, perhaps it's **FEAR.**

Innovation is about courage. Courage to try new things and allow our spirit to soar. People often refuse to innovate because of fear. Fear is a thinking problem. Fear is a perspective problem, and ultimately, the reason we don't innovate is poor perspective.

You see, if I am genuinely committed to obtaining knowledge, I can DIG to find it. If I am committed to gaining more resources, I can DIG to find them. It's not really about either of those, but about a willingness to do the digging. And in my professional opinion, what stops most organizations, families, and individuals from being innovative is FEAR.

FEAR of what?

Failure

Ridicule

Rejection

Standing Out

Unfamiliarity

Restructuring

Greater Responsibility

There is always room for change if we will allow it. Our families, organizations, clients, and customers will tend to have better experiences because of our willingness to renovate and remodel. These changes keep people excited and inspired. Now, is renovation the same as innovation? No, but it is an essential part of it! If we refuse to update our surroundings, it may be because change has been placed low on our priority list.

Company outings, attending team building workshops, or introducing incentive programs to the team are also ways of innovating. If you wait until you are one hundred percent sure of what to do, you'll always be too late. The time to innovate is now.

If we are not changing, we are simply dying. How many times have you heard someone say, "I am just too old to change?" Change is available to all of us, including you.

So, why do people neglect to do this? Because of blind spots! After you have seen something the way it has been for so long, you begin to not pay attention to it. If a light fixture is broken, a ding is in the wall, a desk or table is damaged, over time you stop noticing. The blind spot happens because you have told yourself that change is not essential or has no immediate value. What we do not believe is valuable begins to become blurred out in our minds. Psychologists call it "cognitive tunneling." We lock onto "valuable" things and blur out many of the things that we believe are not. Our office furniture, wardrobe, and our branding can all become overlooked due to a perceived lack of value. If we don't think it is valuable, we tend not to give it much attention. Over time it's as if we are blind in that area. Other people can see it, we cannot.

I was recently invited to visit and tour Dallas Cowboy headquarters in Frisco, Texas, by my friends at Complexity Gaming. Complexity is an online gaming corporation partnered with The Dallas Cowboys. The Cowboys are the most valuable team in the NFL worth an estimated five billion dollars. Touring the facility was mind-blowing! Jerry Jones, the owner of the Dallas Cowboys, is an innovator. He is willing to push the envelope on marketing, branding, merchandise, and virtually anything that represents the Cowboy organization. The offices, restaurants, workout facilities, and training rooms are state-of-the-art. The enormous facility contains marble, glass, and LED touch screens everywhere you look. Superbowl trophies and rings are displayed in cases throughout the facility as well. It's all done with what I would call "over the top" decor. I came home and immediately began investigating my office space and podcast studio, realizing they both needed updating. Is my company a five-billion-dollar organization? No, not yet. But that does not mean I have to wait until I get to that level of success before I upgrade and improve my environment. The truth is, I probably need to be more innovative if I want to create even greater success. When I learned that Jerry Jones arrives to work in a helicopter that lands on the fifty-yard line of the practice field behind his offices, I realized that I think way too small. We all do!

You and I are creatures of habit, and once we lock into a pattern, breaking it can be difficult. For that reason, we must be willing to force ourselves to DIG. Innovation must be a requirement made by us merely because it is so easy to keep doing things like we have done them for so long. The old phrase, "If it isn't broke, we don't need to fix it" comes to mind. However, I think that if it's not broke, and it has been the same for so long that it no longer compels and inspires people, we may NEED to break it.

Abraham Lincoln once said, *"It is what it is, but will become what we make it."*

Holding tightly to what we have always done can suffocate what could be.

Reinventing a marriage is a great way to innovate. I listened to an interview recently where a woman said she had five different marriages, all to the same husband. She and her husband had been willing to change and innovate their relationship for over three decades. That's a great form marriage innovation.

Date nights, gifts, new activities, and vacations to different destinations are all ways of innovating. Developing new routines like getting up earlier to spend quiet time together before the kids wake up is a form of innovation. Going out for coffee or lunch during the day is also a great way to innovate a relationship. It is in the small things we do that can add up to vast improvement.

We must not allow fear or complacency to keep us from dreaming, innovating, and growing. Your family, your team, and your psyche will reward you for being willing to change. There is nothing wrong with you right now, but right now is also a great time to change. Change is good, change is necessary, and change starts within.

The more often we are willing to innovate, the more it becomes a part of who we are.

Robert Iger, CEO of Walt Disney, said, *"It is in our best interest to put some of the old rules aside and create new ones to follow."*

I think of the willingness to innovate like this, *"In the beginning, they will ask you WHY you're doing it? Once you've succeeded, they will ask you HOW you did it."*

I have always been willing to travel to different cities so I can speak to groups and teams. I love being present in the room with individuals as I share with them insights on personal development and transformation. On the other hand, I am pretty sure that I won't always want to travel away from my family to be able do this. For that reason, my team and I have created an innovative way to continue working with organizations without my having to travel to do so. Our DIG Mentorship Program is an online tool where anyone can have access to hundreds of training videos within a monthly membership. It is a phenomenal resource available to leaders like yourself at **www.RonnieDoss.com** and priced so that everyone can afford it. Within this innovative platform, there are videos on relationship building, motivation, conflict resolution, effective communication, sales, team building, and much more. Hours and hours of wisdom and insight are available there to assist families, teams, and individuals to create more powerful results. All of this can be accessed at ANYTIME from a smartphone, tablet, or computer. We are so excited about the new community this resource is helping us to build.

What are you going to do to innovate the areas of your life that need innovating? Are you waiting on all the circumstances to line up or for someone to tell you what you should do? Don't wait! Spend some time strategizing. Just like INTEGRITY is in, so is INNOVATION. If you continue to wait, the opportunity might go to someone else. We will only make a minimal amount of progress doing things the way we have always done.

Innovation is about digging to uncover **new** ways to DIG.

You have one life to live, and this is not the dress rehearsal. The big show is right now, regardless of what has happened in our past. The show must go on, and we must be willing to DIG! Our world is waiting. Put down this book and pick up your shovel. Your time is now.

DIG!

NOTES

CHAPTER ONE
WHO NEEDS TO DIG?

"A champion is not made out of muscle; a champion is made out of heart." **Liang Chow**

CHAPTER TWO
DIGGING FOR WHAT?

"The meaning of life is to find your gift. The purpose of life is to give it away." **Pablo Picasso**

CHAPTER THREE
DIGGING PAST MISCONCEPTIONS

"The belief that there is a point when all the material benefits of the world add up to a general state of happiness is the Great Misconception." **Tarek Saab**

CHAPTER FOUR
DIGGING TOO FAST?

"If you want to go fast go alone, if you want to go far, take some people with you." **African Proverb**

CHAPTER FIVE
TOOLS FOR DIGGING

"Do not wait, the time will never be just right. Start where you stand and work with whatever tools you may have at your command, and better tools will be found as you go along." **George Herbert**

CHAPTER SIX
THE GIFT IN THE DIRT.

"A champion gets up even when he can't." **Unknown**

CHAPTER SEVEN
WHO ARE YOU DIGGING WITH?

"My idea of good company....is the company of clever, well-informed people, who have a great deal of conversation; that is what I call good company." **Jane Austen**

CHAPTER EIGHT
PUTTING DOWN THE SHOVEL.

"Life is the continuous adjustment of internal relations to external relations." **Herbert Spencer**

CHAPTER NINE
DIGGING OUT

"If you are digging a hole in the wrong place, making it deeper will not help."
Seymour Chwast

CHAPTER TEN
GROUNDBREAKING CEREMONY

"It was character that got us out of bed, commitment that moved us into action, and discipline that enabled us to follow through." **Zig Ziglar**

CHAPTER ELEVEN
THE MOST ESSENTIAL SHOVELS.

"Give us the tools, and we will finish the job."
Winston Churchill

Printed in the USA
CPSIA information can be obtained
at www.ICGtesting.com
LVHW011959270124
769657LV00004B/11/J